THE COACHING CORNER

the coaching corner ®

By Sarah Makinde & Co.

THE COACHING CORNER

Copyright © Sarah Makinde & Co.

All rights reserved.

ISBN: 9798307881965

The following chapters are Sarah Makinde & Co's intellectual property and the stories of the individuals. All rights reserved. No part of this book may be reproduced or modified in any form, including photocopying, recording, or by information storage and retrieval system, without written permission from the publisher/author.

Legal Notice: This book is for personal use only. You cannot amend, distribute, sell, use, quote or paraphrase any part of this book's content without the author's or copyright owner's consent. Legal action will be pursued if this is breached. The information provided herein is stated to be truthful and consistent in that any liability, in terms of inattention or otherwise, by any usage or abuse of any policies, processes, or directions contained within is the solitary and utter responsibility of the recipient reader. Under no circumstances will any legal responsibility or blame be held against the publisher for any reparation, damages, or monetary loss due to the information herein, either directly or indirectly.

Disclaimer Notice: The views, opinions, and advice expressed by other authors in this book are solely their own. This book is not providing medical advice; it is intended for informational purposes only. It is not a substitute for professional medical advice, diagnosis or treatment. Never ignore professional medical advice in seeking treatment. Every attempt has been made to provide accurate, up-to-date, reliable, and complete information. No warranties of any kind are expressed or implied. Readers acknowledge that the author is not engaging in the rendering of legal, financial, medical or professional advice. By reading this document, the reader agrees that under no circumstances are we responsible for any losses, direct or indirect, which are incurred as a result of the use of the information contained within this document, including, but not limited to, errors, omissions, or inaccuracies. These stories are written by real people in their own words.

THE COACHING CORNER

Dedication

To everyone who continues to help others grow while growing themselves.

This book is dedicated to the changemakers, the dreamers, and the doers—the ones who show up every day to create impact and transformation in their own lives and the lives of others.

To my family, friends, and The Coaching Corner® community who have supported me on my journey—you mean so much to me. And to every client, coach, therapist, and professional who has trusted me to be part of your story—this is for you.

With gratitude and love as always,
Sarah

THE COACHING CORNER

THE COACHING CORNER

Contents

Foreword By **Sarah Makinde**	Page: 7
Chapter 1: **Sarah Makinde**	Page: 9
Chapter 2: **Lucie Reveco**	Page: 21
Chapter 3: **Andreas Dating Coach**	Page: 37
Chapter 4: **Linda Robinson**	Page: 55
Chapter 5: **Skylar Acamesis**	Page: 71
Chapter 6: **Dr Suzanne Henwood**	Page: 81
Chapter 7: **Ian Norton**	Page: 99
Chapter 8: **Ashley Harrison**	Page: 113
Chapter 9: **Sarah Creevey**	Page: 133
Chapter 10: **Katy Walton**	Page: 149
Chapter 11: **Jennifer Anderson**	Page: 165
Chapter 12: **Kelly Watts**	Page: 181
Chapter 13: **Heather Rosewood**	Page: 193
Chapter 14: **Sarah Luke**	Page: 205
Chapter 15: **Noor Aishah**	Page: 219
Chapter 16: **Ghazali Abdul Wahab**	Page: 235
Chapter 17: **Amy Fong**	Page: 249
Chapter 18: **Elsa Farouz-Fouquet**	Page: 261
Chapter 19: **Emma Leivesley**	Page: 277
Chapter 20: **Vicky Regan**	Page: 291

THE COACHING CORNER

THE COACHING CORNER

Foreword

By Sarah Makinde

This book is for you, the changemakers. The ones who support others whether this is formally or informally. The ones who are looking to learn coaching tools to help themselves through their own challenges. The ones who are simply looking to make a difference in the world.

I've poured everything into this—20+ years of HR and occupational psychology experience, lessons from my own journey as a coach and NLP trainer, and the insights I've gained working with thousands of people like you who are passionate about helping others.

It's not just a guide; it's your toolkit, your motivator, and your reminder that transformation starts with you. So, grab a cup of tea (or your beverage of choice), settle in, and let's dive into this next

THE COACHING CORNER

chapter of your journey. You've got this—and I'm here cheering you on every step of the way.

With love and belief in you and your gift to the world,
Sarah

THE COACHING CORNER

Chapter 1

My Journey to Discovering Strength in Uniqueness

By Sarah Makinde

I often used to ask myself: if I were to start my life over again, would I do things differently?

Many years ago, the answer to this question would have been a resounding yes. Yet today, the answer is a most definite no.

You see, the dots have connected – my childhood, the trauma, the moments when life felt unbearably hard. My pain, my joy, my tears, my scars. All of it has led me to where I am now: running multiple businesses, leading a thriving community of over 18,000 incredible people, living in a house that I am renovating and I'm proud to call my own home, and surrounding myself with family and friends who love me for who I truly am.

THE COACHING CORNER

This reflection often makes me wonder what was different back then compared to now. What tools and insights helped me get here? To a place where life isn't just worth living but worth living well – as my authentic self, without losing myself trying to please others. This chapter is my story of transformation, of finding strength in my uniqueness, and of building The Coaching Corner® - a group with over 18,000 other members with one desire - to help others in any way possible.

The Dots That Connected My Journey

When I reflect on the path that brought me to where I am today, it feels like tracing the intricate patterns of a kaleidoscope—beautiful yet unpredictable, with every turn offering a new perspective. It wasn't always easy to see the beauty in it, though. For much of my life, I felt lost in a maze of challenges, carrying labels that felt like heavy chains: teenage mum, not good enough, outsider. Yet, these very struggles became the seeds of resilience, shaping the person I am today and inspiring the work I do now.

I grew up feeling different, caught between cultures, between expectations, and with, what felt like, the weight of societal judgments on my shoulders. As a young girl born in Nigeria and raised in the UK, I often felt like I belonged nowhere and like I didn't fit in. By the time I was 15, I had left home, which meant the differences just grew bigger between me and my many peers still living with their parents. At 18, I became a mother—a moment that was both the most terrifying and transformative of my life, resulting in an even bigger difference between me and my peers. Whilst my friends were planning their prom, I was saving for a pram. Society had already decided what my future would look like, and they weren't afraid to tell me that I was a disappointment, a burden and an outcast. Some people saw me as a statistic, a cautionary tale, someone destined to struggle. And struggle I did, but not in the way they expected.

The criticism and cynicism fuelled my fire. I pushed myself relentlessly, often to my breaking point, determined to rewrite the narrative imposed on me. Studying for A-levels while raising a baby. Working five jobs while pursuing a master's degree. Sacrificing time with my son to build a career, prove my worth, and chase a vision of success that wasn't even my own.

At the time, I thought I was proving something to the world, but in reality, I was desperately trying to prove something to myself. It wasn't the derogatory labels that other people gave to me that hurt the most. It was the words I was saying to myself, that I didn't realise were the most damaging. I wanted to believe I was enough. But no matter how much I achieved, it never felt like it. Pride? Accomplishment? Those words felt foreign to me. I was exhausted, burned out, and lost.

No matter how much I achieved, it wasn't enough - it never quite filled this huge hole of not feeling good enough. What I thought was my superpower - hard work, determination and grit. Soon felt like my kryptonite - eventually leading me to my breakdown.

THE COACHING CORNER

Losing Myself to Find Myself

"The wound is the place where the light enters you." – Rumi

It took years for me to realise that in my quest to meet everyone else's expectations, I had completely abandoned my own. I didn't know who I was anymore. I had become a chameleon, adapting to fit in, to be accepted, to avoid rejection. Straightening my hair to look more "professional." Softening my voice to seem less assertive. Smiling through pain to maintain the illusion of having it all together. Each compromise took me further from myself.

Then came the cracks—moments of overwhelm, anxiety, and depression that forced me to pause and confront the truth. I realised that I couldn't keep running on empty. I didn't want a life half lived. Not knowing who I was at the end of it and having so many regrets. Too late to do anything to change it. It felt like the wounds I had managed to stick a plaster over - the self-loathing, the low self-esteem, the desire to be anyone but myself, began to open up. The pain felt unbearable - like a tsunami of emotions that hit me all at once.

I didn't want to be still. Being still felt alien to me. But I had no choice - my body and mind gave up. As a result of a breakdown and choosing to take voluntary redundancy over losing my health and happiness - I was forced to be still.

It was in these moments of stillness, painful as they were, that I began to rebuild. Slowly, I started to peel back the layers of societal conditioning and self-doubt. Mindfulness became my lifeline, teaching me to sit with my thoughts rather than run from them. I learned to notice my emotions without judgment, to let go of the stories I'd told myself about who I was and what I was capable of. It was in these moments I realised who I had become, and who I wanted to be. I still get tearful now thinking about how many more years I would have lived in this way - not knowing who I was. Looking happy but not being happy. Feeling so unfulfilled. When I discovered my strengths, my uniqueness and how I could use this to be even more me and create even more meaning in my life and in the world, it was the key that unlocked the prison that I had created for myself.

The Fire That Transformed Me

There's a quote by Viktor Frankl that has stayed with me: "What is to give light must endure burning." That fire—the pain, the struggle, the relentless pursuit of "enough"—was what ultimately transformed me. It burned away the false narratives and left behind a clarity I hadn't known before. I stopped striving for validation from others and started seeking fulfillment within myself. I began to understand that my worth was not something to be earned or proven; it was inherent. I, like everyone else, was put on this earth for a purpose. I am here for a reason. It is in my uniqueness that I can find my strength.

This realisation became the foundation of my business and my mission: to help others see their worth, break free from the labels

THE COACHING CORNER

that limit them, and embrace their authentic selves. Whether it's through coaching, training, or community-building, my work is rooted in the belief that everyone deserves to feel seen, heard, and valued—just as they are.

When you join the coaching corner® community, you will see a community that thrives on differences. You do not need to be like everyone else - being different is your superpower.

> *"To be yourself in a world that is constantly trying to make you something else is the greatest accomplishment."* – Ralph Waldo Emerson

A Kaleidoscope of Gratitude

Over the past year, I've achieved things I once thought impossible. Growing my business to six figures. Building a community of over 18,000 people. Purchasing another property and working with other entrepreneurs on a similar mission with shared values. But what matters most to me isn't the external success; it's the internal peace I've found along the way. For the first time, I feel proud—not because of what I've achieved, but because of who I've become.

Every twist and turn, every challenge and triumph, has contributed to the person I am today. I've learned to embrace my story—all of it—as a source of strength rather than shame. The labels that once weighed me down have become reminders of my resilience. Teenage mum? Yes, and that taught me tenacity. Outsider? Perhaps, but that gave me empathy. Not good enough? On the contrary, I am enough, just as I am.

THE COACHING CORNER

Reframing my situation has been an important part of my journey. As human beings we have a negativity bias. Just think of a moment where something happened, and it became so easy to almost get obsessed with the negative aspects of the situation. This is normal - it can take a lot to focus on the positive, or even the learnings from the situation. However, this comes easier with practice - just like building a mental muscle. If we do this more, it will become more natural.

I could quite easily sit here and dwell on my past, the mistakes I have made (believe me I have made many), the paths that I wish I hadn't taken, but how helpful would that be? Sometimes what seems easier is not the best solution in the long run.

I am not into toxic positivity and ignoring the pain, challenges and disappointments and just sticking a plaster over everything and covering it with a smile. Why? Because the cracks will appear at some stage, whether this is with my family, friends, relationships, or my own health. I am all about recognising the emotion, exploring the feeling and taking the learnings and looking at what I can do differently next time - I have found this most helpful across many situations.

Believe me, I have been through some dark times and times of not wanting to be here because life just seems too hard. If it wasn't for reframing and gratitude, there are many situations that would have felt too hard to bring myself back from.

THE COACHING CORNER

Lived Experience Is Your Superpower

I never really talk about the educational accolades and titles I have achieved across the years after my name. I always chased the next level, not because I particularly enjoyed the learning. It was the thought that the next thing I did would make me feel more confident. If only I could get that next title, then perhaps then I would feel like I was worthy enough to put myself out there and start my business. It just felt like another mask I was putting on in the hope that the next mask would help me realise who I was, what I was passionate about and what my purpose was.

These accolades helped create a screen that I could hide behind – although I didn't feel like I had achieved much as the titles didn't bring me joy. Society seemed to celebrate them. I hid my past with these titles in fear that people would judge me and make me feel even less than I felt already. I hid who I really was and how I felt about things. I let others overstep boundaries because it didn't feel like what I wanted mattered, or how I felt counted for anything.

Eventually things changed. I began to find joy in education and learning – not because it made me feel more confident, but because learning had always been something that energised me, which became so apparent when I changed the meaning I gave it. What I soon realised is that the degrees, masters etc were great and gave me credibility in my field. They showed that I had a certain level of knowledge. But it was the things I kept hidden – my experience, my story and my vulnerability that people connected with more than my titles. It was when I truly stepped into who I was, and what made me unique, that my business began to grow.

The story that I had been fearful of people finding out for so many years – my coming from Nigeria with nothing but a suitcase, my leaving home at 15, my getting pregnant at 18, my breakdown, my redundancy. I thought it was a weakness and a flaw – something that meant I didn't fit in. When in reality it was my uniqueness that was the thing that drove me, the thing that kept me humble, and the things that helped people connect with me.

So, Would I Do Things Differently?

As I reflect on the beginning of the story and the question about whether or not, if I started my life over again, I would do things differently. I love that my answer would be no. It's taken me so many years to get to this point and to realise that my greatest challenges are also my greatest achievements.

I came across the following quote from Marianne Williamson, which I love, and sums up my story well:

"Our deepest fear is not that we are inadequate. Our deepest fear is that we are powerful beyond measure. It is our light, not our darkness, that most frightens us. We ask ourselves, 'Who am I to be brilliant, gorgeous, talented, fabulous?' Actually, who are you not to be?"

THE COACHING CORNER

As we come to the end of my story, I ask you: Who are you not to be amazing? Who are you not to be great? Who are you not to be YOU?

To be anyone else and to dim your light is to deprive the world of your beauty, your talent, and your greatness.

As I look back on my life, I'm grateful for every twist and turn. Each challenge, each triumph, each lesson has brought me here. And now, I'm committed to helping others discover their own strength, embrace their uniqueness, and live lives full of purpose and joy.

This is my story. And I can't wait to hear yours.

Your Journey Starts Here

If my story resonates with you, if you see parts of yourself in my journey, I invite you to take the next step. The Coaching Corner® Community is here to support you. It's a space where you can:

- Discover your strengths and use them to create a life you love.
- Learn practical tools to build confidence and overcome challenges.
- Get your coaching hours to contribute towards your certification.
- Connect with a community of people who will uplift and inspire you.

THE COACHING CORNER

Your uniqueness is your superpower. And the world needs what only you can offer. Join us at **The Coaching Corner®** and start your journey today. Let's grow together, transform together, and create meaningful impact.

Visit **The Coaching Corner® Community** to learn more and join us now.

THE COACHING CORNER

THE COACHING CORNER

Chapter 2

By Lucie Reveco

NLP Ambassador & Trainer, therapist and professional coach

The Brain's Hidden Playbook

At our very core, we are love itself. Love forms the foundation of every part of our lives. As my professor, Patrik Maturkanic, so aptly says, *"Every individual craves love, for they are innately crafted for it."* Yet, to truly embrace love, we must first release the negative emotions that quietly accumulate in our subconscious, often holding us back. Emotions like anger, sadness, fear, guilt, and hurt become hidden obstacles, quietly keeping us from experiencing the depth of love we're meant to enjoy.

These emotions have been our teachers, each imparting lessons that have shaped us. But there comes a moment when we must acknowledge their purpose, thank them, and gently let them go.

THE COACHING CORNER

Only then can we fully open ourselves to a life filled with love and alignment. When we embrace love within ourselves, it radiates outward, enriching our thoughts, actions, and relationships, fostering a life of harmony, resilience, and joy. This journey towards love, both for ourselves and others, is a return to the essence that truly defines us.

The Brain's Hidden Playbook serves as a guide to understanding the powerful and often mysterious part of our minds known as the subconscious. Beneath our everyday thoughts and actions, the subconscious mind runs like a hidden operating system, influencing everything we do—from our habits to our deepest-held beliefs. It quietly shapes our decisions, often without us realising it.

Imagine the subconscious as your brain's hidden playbook, filled with old scripts that we follow without knowing. These scripts are shaped by past experiences, especially those from childhood, and they often repeat the same unhelpful messages: *"I'm not good enough"* or *"I don't deserve success."* While some of these scripts protect us, others hold us back. The good news? We have the power to rewrite them.

In this chapter, you'll explore tools like NLP Time Line Therapy®, Inner Kindness & Self-Questioning, and the Power of Three Guardians. These methods allow us to discover and transform the underlying patterns of thought and feeling that guide our lives, empowering us to create new, positive beliefs. Imagine the

THE COACHING CORNER

freedom of replacing outdated mental habits with ones that truly support who you are today.

Hi, my name is Lucie. For years, I carried the weight of my past—shaped by childhood trauma that left me feeling broken and disconnected. Healing wasn't easy, but it taught me one of life's most profound lessons: we all have the power to rewrite our story. Through neurolinguistic programming, studies in psychology, and self-compassion, I found my way back to myself—and discovered tools to transform not just my life but the lives of others.

Today, I am a successful woman, a happy mum of two, and a loving wife. I live a high-quality life filled with purpose and joy, empowering individuals and corporate clients to embark on their own transformative journeys. My mission is to help people understand their pain, reconnect with their inner strength, and step into the lives they've always dreamed of.

In my chapter The Brain's Hidden Playbook, I invite you to explore the mysterious yet fascinating mechanisms of your subconscious mind. It's where silent, automatic patterns guide your emotions, decisions, and even your perception of success. How does your mind choose which beliefs to nurture? Why do some habits feel impossible to break? And most importantly, how can you take control of this hidden playbook to shape the life you truly desire? This chapter isn't just a deep dive into neuroscience and psychology; it's your roadmap to transformation. Together, we'll uncover the keys to rewriting the scripts holding you back,

THE COACHING CORNER

unlocking your mind's full potential, and creating a life aligned with your truest self.

Are you ready to step into the hidden world of your mind? Let's uncover the playbook and begin the adventure of a lifetime.

NLP Time Line Therapy® – Releasing the Past, Embracing the Future

Imagine our life as a necklace of pearls. Each pearl on the necklace represents a memory, an experience, or an event from our past, present, or even our envisioned future. This is the essence of Time Line Therapy®—seeing life events, like pearls on a necklace, strung together to make up who we are.

In Time Line Therapy®, a technique within Neuro-Linguistic Programming (NLP), we can work with these "pearls" to improve our well-being, release burdens, and reach our goals.

Principles of Time Line Therapy®

Time Line Therapy® is based on several guiding ideas:

1. **Everyone Experiences Time Differently**

Just as everyone's necklace of memories and experiences looks a bit different, each of us experiences the passage of time in our own way. This unique sense of time affects how we think, feel, and act.

THE COACHING CORNER

2. Memories Are Like Pearls on a Strand

Our memories do not float randomly in our minds. They are stored along a "strand" or "timeline," much like pearls on a necklace. This line represents our life's journey and personal history, where each pearl captures an experience that contributes to who we are today.

3. Emotions Are Connected to Past Events

Some pearls are smooth and shiny, symbolising joyful moments, while others might feel heavier, carrying the weight of sadness, anger, or regret. Time Line Therapy® helps us let go of the negative emotions tied to specific memories, allowing us to appreciate the necklace as a whole and leave the painful feelings behind.

4. The Power of the Unconscious Mind

The unconscious mind is like the clasp holding our necklace together, a place where much of our inner strength resides. By accessing this part of ourselves, we can find new ways to let go of what weighs us down and move forward in peace and confidence.

Finding Your Pearl Necklace of Memories (Eliciting the Timeline)

In Time Line Therapy®, one of the first steps is to locate and understand your inner "necklace" of memories. This involves exploring where you mentally "see" or "feel" your past, present, and future.

- "Where do you see the pearls representing your past?"
- "Where do you place your future on this necklace?"

THE COACHING CORNER

- "What is your sense of the present moment?"

Letting Go of Past Burdens (Clearing the Past)

Time Line Therapy® allows us to clear away the heavy feelings that may be tied to some "pearls" on our necklace. By doing this, we release old emotions and limiting beliefs that may be holding us back. Imagine revisiting a difficult moment in your past, one of those heavier pearls. In Time Line Therapy®, the practitioner gently guides you through a process of reframing this memory, seeing it from a fresh perspective. This might involve forgiving yourself or someone else, letting go of an emotional attachment, or simply shifting how you view that experience. Gradually, this pearl becomes lighter, its burden lifted, allowing you to move forward more freely.

Strengthening the Strand with Future Goals (Empowering the Future)

Time Line Therapy® does not stop at clearing away old emotions—it helps us look toward the future also. Just as we can choose beautiful new pearls to add to a necklace, we can set meaningful goals and visualise the life we desire. In this part of the therapy, you are guided to picture your ideal future. Think of it as selecting the most precious pearls to add to your strand. You might imagine your future goals vividly, sensing the confidence and happiness you will feel upon achieving them. This process of

THE COACHING CORNER

mentally rehearsing success makes it easier to move toward your dreams with clarity and determination.

Finding Harmony in the Present (Structuring the Present)

Balancing the pearls on our necklace, from past to future, also means that we need harmony in the present. Structuring the present is about ensuring that our thoughts, emotions, and actions align with who we truly are and what we want. A practitioner can help you spot any areas where your current thoughts or feelings may not align with your goals. Perhaps there are two conflicting "pearls" representing decisions or emotions that do not feel right together. Through Time Line Therapy®, these elements can be harmonised, helping you become a more integrated, balanced version of yourself, where all aspects flow naturally and contribute to a meaningful life.

A Gentle Guide to Releasing Emotions with Time Line Therapy®

This guide provides a step-by-step approach to working through emotions or limiting beliefs that may be holding you back. Take each step slowly, allowing your subconscious mind to guide you at a comfortable pace.

1. Seek Permission from Your Unconscious Mind

Begin by asking yourself:
"Is it all right for my unconscious mind to release this emotion or belief today, and for me to be aware of it consciously?"

THE COACHING CORNER

(Pause for a moment and feel a sense of readiness.)

2. Gently Travel to the Root of the Issue

Allow yourself to feel guided back to the earliest time that connects with this issue.

"Let this feeling, thought, or memory take me back to the very first instance that, once accessed, will help me re-evaluate and resolve this issue."

When you feel you have reached that memory, gently nod or take a moment to acknowledge it.

3. Invite Learnings from the Experience

Ask your unconscious mind:

"What do I need to learn from this experience to release these emotions easily and naturally?"

(Pause and notice any insights or feelings that arise. When you are ready, summarise them to yourself.)

4. Offer Support to Your Younger Self

Imagine seeing your younger self in that memory and extending to them the wisdom and reassurance you now possess.

"What did my younger self need? Let me give them all the strength and insights I have today."

5. Reframe the Experience with a New Perspective

Ask yourself:

"How does this old issue appear to me now? What fresh perspectives can I see that might help it shift?"

You might imagine viewing the scene from different angles, perhaps as an observer or from above, to gain new insights.

THE COACHING CORNER

6. Check for a Sense of Completion

Ask yourself if this memory feels resolved.

"Is this memory complete for me now, or does something else still need attention?"

If there is more, allow your mind to guide you to any other related memories.

7. Apply the Learnings Across Your Timeline

If all memories feel resolved, gently suggest to yourself:

"I will allow these positive learnings to travel across my timeline, enriching every memory that might benefit from them."

Imagine these insights reaching every part of you, from head to toe.

8. Visualise the Change in the Future

Picture yourself moving forward in time with these new changes firmly in place. Notice how they shape and uplift your future self.

"How does this change feel as I move into my future now?"

At the end of the session, you should feel clearer, more focused, and empowered to make the changes you desire. Time Line Therapy® is a wonderful approach to creating peace and balance in your life. By understanding and transforming your own "pearl necklace" of memories, you gain control over the experiences that shape you and can walk confidently toward the future you wish to create.

Whether working with a practitioner or exploring the principles on your own, Time Line Therapy® offers valuable insights that can

THE COACHING CORNER

guide your personal growth and happiness.

> *"Lucie Reveco is the true essence of NLP—bringing passion and a profoundly human approach to every lesson. Her lectures don't just inform; they inspire with authenticity, as Lucie lives every principle she teaches. Her humility and deep respect for each student, whether in one-on-one sessions or group coaching, leave an unforgettable impression. Cooperating with Lucie is a transformative experience."*
> – Dr. Katerina Dolezalova

Inner Kindness and Self-Questioning

"I discovered that you can teach an old dog new tricks; therefore, you can teach people new things," says Richard Bandler, and this could not be truer when it comes to learning the art of inner kindness. Cultivating kindness towards ourselves is an essential step in understanding our emotions, gaining genuine insights, and moving forward with purpose. This chapter delves into how we can nurture self-compassion through gentle self-questioning and mindful reflection, laying a foundation for authentic healing and growth.

By learning to speak to ourselves as we would a dear friend, especially during difficult times, we embrace self-compassion as a powerful support. Using patient and empathetic language, we not only honour our feelings but actively shape a life of joy and resilience. When we take the time to truly listen to our needs, our bodies, and our experiences, we foster a kinder relationship with ourselves, opening the door to both emotional and physical well-being. This practice of inner kindness brings us to a more balanced, joyful life, reminding us that we are not only capable of change but also wholly deserving of it.

Guiding Questions for Self-Discovery

1. What am I not seeing yet?

This question invites us to pause and consider any hidden aspects of a situation. Often, we are too close to events or emotions to see the full picture. By asking what remains unseen, we open ourselves to new perspectives and unspoken truths, allowing deeper self-awareness to arise.

2. What is love asking from me?

Love, as a guiding force, often calls us to act with patience, understanding, or courage. When we question what love might be asking, we are better prepared to respond with gentleness toward ourselves and others, making space for healing and compassion.

3. How did I get to this situation?

Reflecting on how we arrived at our current state can illuminate choices, actions, and patterns that may have led us here. This is not about blame; it is a tool for growth. Understanding our journey helps us make different choices in the future.

4. What have I learned?

Every experience offers us a lesson, even if it is one we would rather avoid. This question helps us identify those learnings and transform them into wisdom that we can carry forward, turning each difficulty into a stepping stone.

THE COACHING CORNER

5. What can I do so I am not in this situation again?

By considering what we can do differently, we become empowered. This is not about suppressing emotions but understanding how to act in ways that align with our values and lead to positive outcomes.

6. What is the positive outcome of my current situation?

Even a challenging situation holds a positive side, however small. Finding this silver lining encourages resilience, helping us see that every experience, no matter how tough, has something valuable to offer.

7. What is my emotion telling me? Why did it come?

Emotions serve as messengers. When we ask what an emotion is trying to communicate, we get closer to understanding our needs and boundaries, fostering a healthier relationship with our inner world.

8. What is the emotion teaching me?

Each emotion holds a lesson—anger might show us where a boundary needs to be set, while sadness might teach us about acceptance. By learning from our emotions, we build emotional resilience and become more self-aware.

> "I am genuinely grateful for my collaboration with Lucie, which has brought tremendous growth to my life. Together, we've uncovered my inner strength and tackled the challenges that seemed to reappear time and again. Embracing change takes courage, but every step of this journey has been worth it. Lucie is like an angel who's entered my life, creating a wonderful partnership filled with support, joy, and growth." - Martina Valuskova

THE COACHING CORNER

The Power of the Three Guardians

Our thoughts, mental images, and inner voices act as powerful guides, shaping our emotions, decisions, and the way we experience life. These "Three Guardians" have a profound influence on our reality, impacting not only how we feel but also the choices we make and the paths we pursue. As Dr. Milton Erickson insightfully noted, *"Life will bring you pain all by itself. Our responsibility is to create joy."* Understanding the power of these inner elements gives us the tools to do just that, allowing us to create a life that is compassionate, resilient, and joyful.

To fully harness the potential of the Three Guardians, we need to be mindful of the language we use within ourselves. Language provides the foundation for coding our experiences, communicating with our inner self, and guiding our internal dialogue each day.

Often, our inner voice mirrors the tone we grew up with, perhaps echoing the voices of parents or caregivers, until we make a conscious choice to shape it ourselves. By learning to use our thoughts, images, and inner voice constructively, we can gently influence how we interpret our experiences, encouraging us to face challenges with a spirit of joy and freedom. As Dr. Richard Bandler reminds us, *"Freedom is everything, and love is all the rest."* Embracing these principles, we can build a life that is both meaningful and rich with inner peace.

THE COACHING CORNER

The Influence of Thoughts, Images, and Inner Voice

All learning occurs unconsciously, which means that by bringing awareness to our thoughts, mental images, and the tone of our inner voice, we can actively shape a more supportive inner world.

Thoughts: Our thoughts function like seeds planted in our minds; they can be repetitive, critical, or uplifting. Negative thoughts often deepen feelings of sadness or anxiety, preventing us from moving forward. Conversely, positive and affirming thoughts can elevate our spirits, instilling a sense of capability and confidence. By consciously choosing to focus on supportive thoughts, we lay a solid foundation for self-acceptance and resilience. Remember, it is not the problems themselves that hold us back; rather, it is our perception of those problems. When we shift our focus to solutions and trust in our abilities, our subconscious mind can guide us to opportunities and insights that help resolve our challenges. We are in control of our minds and our thoughts, and we have the power to change them.

Inner Images: The mental images we hold play a significant role in shaping our emotional responses. Positive visualisations can provide comfort and inspiration, fostering hope and clarity. In contrast, negative or fear-inducing images often lead to stress and hesitation. To enhance our ability to confront challenges with composure, it is helpful to cultivate positive mental images. If you find yourself burdened by negative memories or images, try this NLP exercise from Dr. Richard Bandler:

THE COACHING CORNER

1. **Identify the Memory:** Recall a recent event that still bothers you—something you wish to let go of. Visualise this memory as a film in your mind's eye.
2. **Shrink the Image:** Make the image smaller and push it into the distance, draining its colour and brightness.
3. **Fade the Sounds:** If you can hear sounds or voices from this scene, allow them to fade away.
4. **Blur the Image:** Make the image so small that you have to squint to see it clearly and then reduce it even further.
5. **Brush It Away:** When the image is the size of a breadcrumb, simply brush it away.

Inner Voice: Perhaps the most influential of the Three Guardians is our inner voice. The tone and language we use when speaking to ourselves can either empower us or overwhelm us. A critical inner voice can make life's challenges seem insurmountable, while a gentle, encouraging voice acts as a supportive friend, guiding us through difficulties with poise and assurance. Recognising that we can change our inner dialogue empowers us to let it resonate with love, compassion, and encouragement. Behind every negative self-talk lies a positive secondary gain that serves the needs of our subconscious mind. To explore this, ask your inner voice: What is the positive secondary gain of this tone? What is its highest positive intention? Once your subconscious mind provides an answer, choose to replace that negative tone with something more pleasurable or loving.

THE COACHING CORNER

"Through this collaboration, I discovered a deeper understanding of myself, learned to make choices aligned with who I truly am, and gained fresh insights into how others think and act. It's been an incredibly empowering and enlightening journey."
-Assoc. Prof. Ing. Milan Fila, Ph.D.

Thank you for taking the time and courage to explore this chapter with me. I hope it has offered you valuable insights and inspiration on your journey toward self-discovery and growth. If you are interested in collaborating or wish to deepen your understanding of NLP, I invite you to get in touch with me. Together, we can explore the transformative power of these techniques and how they can enhance your personal and professional life.

Your journey towards becoming an NLP practitioner can be a fulfilling and enriching experience, filled with opportunities for learning and connection. I look forward to the possibility of working together and supporting you as you embark on this exciting path. Let's nurture our shared passion for growth and transformation.

Website: https://en.reveco.me

Facebook / Instagram / LinkedIn:
www.linktr.ee/luciereveco

THE COACHING CORNER

Chapter 3

By Andreas

Dating & Relationship Coach

Circology – A New Perspective on Compatibility

I'm assuming you're reading this in a quiet and calm space. Try to clear your mind of any distractions and take a few deep breaths before you read on.

When you're ready, I invite you to:

Imagine you're at a circus... Imagine the lights, the sounds, the smells, the fun, the laughter, the thrills, and the suspense... Now, close your eyes for a moment and imagine: which act or performer would you be, and why?

It's very important to write down your answer while it's fresh in your mind, in as much detail as possible. Its significance will become

THE COACHING CORNER

clear, but I want you to have your role selected before you proceed; if you need a moment to reflect on your choice, please do so now.

Dating is a process of interviews to fill the position of Lover, Soulmate, Partner, Husband, Wife, Companion, Confidant, etc. for as long as you can tolerate each other!

Growing up, I truly believed in the forever dream and marriage, and for me, that statement above read "for life!" Instead, I've witnessed the transition from life to something much more pessimistic and time stamped. We now think in terms of how long, rather than forever. I think it's a shame. Of course, there are many relationships that need to end for the good of both partners, and it's never been easier to do so. Statistically, more serious relationships end in breakups than stay together. I've been through this several times indeed. It's a painful experience, but luckily for me, there were no children involved. It can be financially crippling and emotionally demanding. The fear of going through it again deters most people for life!

Successful modern dating relies on a stronger foundation than ever before. Identifying your ideal relationship dynamic through open, honest, and authentic communication is essential and should be shared by both partners to reveal compatibility; they go hand in hand. Today, the dating world, primarily in online spaces like dating sites, seems to be full of deceit, a lack of respect, openness, and communication. Ghosting, where potential partners vanish to avoid confrontation, is purely disrespectful. Whatever the excuse or motivation, it's essential to strive for transparency and

THE COACHING CORNER

kindness to foster healthier dating environments. This process creates resentment and frustration, and you can feel the anger when you talk to singles.

When I found myself navigating the world of online dating, I posed a crucial question: How do I find "the one," and do they even exist? Dating apps present a plethora of choices, each with potential at first glance. So, how can I avoid the pitfall of investing time and money in endless dates or, worse, finding myself in a toxic relationship with all its negative consequences?

I devised The Circus Question—a single, simple question that could provide the insight I needed.

The Compatibility Tool

Relationship dynamics are more important than ever before. They're the foundation we build upon with our partner, growing in the same direction and evolving together.

By now, you've answered The Circus Question and chosen your role! This exercise isn't just whimsical; it offers a glimpse into your relationship dynamics. The question employs the circus as an analogy, allowing you to unconsciously select your role from the array of relationships, all under the conscious location of the circus tent; simultaneously revealing the role of your ideal partner.

In today's complex dating scene, discerning who deserves your attention and who doesn't is crucial to saving time, and heartache, and may be the key to avoiding toxicity, ensuring your well-being.

THE COACHING CORNER

Having such an advantage in the dating game is undeniably beneficial!

The question provides a simple, efficient, and unintimidating way to filter potential dates. Imagine being able to quickly identify their positive and negative character traits and assess if they align with yours. The feedback from their answer is enlightening, offering an instant overview of their ideal dynamic and whether it complements yours.

Some circus relationship analogies are obvious, like the Lion Tamer and their Lion, the Magician and their Assistant, and the Trapeze Flyer and Catcher. But what about others like the Clown, the Popcorn Seller, or even the Activist who opposes the circus—who are their ideal partners? And that's not all; there are over fifty different choices.

So, what does The Circus Question reveal about relationship dynamics?

It's a Polarity Spectrum

There are two key elements I have discovered that impact your role with a partner and have significant consequences for your relationship dynamics. Both exist on a Polarity Spectrum: the first being power dynamics, and the second, masculine and feminine essence. We each have our ideal dynamic and role to consider when we match with a partner for that balanced dynamic to work. So, let's consider both and what they mean for us.

THE COACHING CORNER

The Balance of Power is Not the Abuse of Power

The intricate power play in relationships is a fascinating subject with significant implications for how we connect with each other. To truly understand this dynamic is to appreciate how it shapes our interactions and, ultimately, our happiness.

"Everything in the world is about sex except sex. Sex is about power."

This familiar quote, often misattributed to Oscar Wilde, serves as a provocative entry point into the conversation about power dynamics within relationships. In today's world, where sexual imagery and themes permeate the media, the link between sex and power has grown even more pronounced. The word "power" in this context extends beyond government and societal laws restricting sexual freedom, tapping into the realm of personal relationships, the dance of dominance and submission.

In my experience, every relational exchange is subtly governed by a balance of power. Not traditionally a tangible metric that can be quantified, but rather an energy that can be identified and qualified by the roles people naturally gravitate towards. Labels like "Dominant," "Submissive," "Switch," "Equal," "Top," and "Bottom" are words society uses to describe these roles, especially pertaining to sexual dynamics in the bedroom. However, the substance of these relationships is not about the roles themselves but the comfort and consent within them. Misunderstanding this, often due to societal misjudgements, leads individuals to associate power in relationships with conflict and negativity; a misguided

THE COACHING CORNER

conclusion that overlooks the potential for consensual, healthy exchanges of power.

The Circus Question identifies your position within the spectrum, confirming what you may already know; if you need to lead, share, or be led in your ideal relationship dynamic. By doing so, it identifies your ideal match in that power dynamic and, very importantly, whom to avoid.

A harmonious relationship does not suffer from a power struggle but thrives on a power exchange that both parties' consent to. This distinction is crucial. Without consent, the potential for emotional damage increases and can result in resentment and dissatisfaction. To successfully navigate personal dynamics, one must reject being coerced into roles that don't align with their authentic selves, for doing so inevitably leads to friction, as many stories of discord and constant conflict will attest.

An understanding of these dynamics is vital, particularly in a society that often equates dominance with strength and submission with weakness. This misconceived hierarchy doesn't hold true in the modern tapestry of human connection. If you find joy in submission, willingly serving your partner without diminishing your self-worth, such a dynamic can bring profound satisfaction. Similarly, if you're naturally inclined to lead, seeking a compatible, consenting partner affords a balanced play of power that can enrich both parties. The challenge lies in shedding historical abuses associated with these dynamics and embracing roles that foster your happiness and fulfilment.

THE COACHING CORNER

It is also essential to disentangle these dynamics from our broader social contexts, such as workplace hierarchies or external interactions, where roles can differ significantly. Many find that while they may hold positions of power in their professional lives, their personal relationships thrive on different terms. The evolution of modern relationship dynamics, particularly over the last century, has seen greater acceptance of diverse power dynamics, promoting balance as a positive and empowering reality rather than a restrictive expectation.

The feminist movement significantly contributed to redefining these roles, advocating for balance and equality both within and outside personal relationships. This has allowed a proliferation of role-sharing in relationships, where partners are free to choose based on personal preferences rather than traditional expectations, thus embracing a true sense of equality.

The phrase "Balance of power is not abuse of power" captures a pivotal truth: healthy relationship dynamics are built on a foundation of mutual respect and consent, without crossing into coercion or unhealthy dominance. Understanding this allows for the crafting of symbiotic partnerships where either shared leadership or a clear delineation of roles suits both individuals' needs.

Crucial to maintaining this balance is open communication. An adaptable relationship, one that can pivot around the evolving dynamics of power, is often the most successful. As individuals evolve, so too do their relational needs, underscoring the

THE COACHING CORNER

transformative nature of relationships. This might mean renegotiating roles or responsibilities, reflecting growth and an ever-deepening bond between partners. This will only happen when both partners are compatibly growing in the same direction from a strong foundation. If mismatched, they will drift apart and lose each other.

Cultural perceptions and societal standards also profoundly influence individual views on power dynamics. Acknowledging these factors can illuminate why certain dynamics resonate more with some than others, emphasising that the goal is a relationship that nurtures the well-being of all involved.

Moreover, the key to maintaining this balance lies in open communication and mutual respect. Whether a couple prefers a single leader or a shared approach, the success of their relationship depends on both parties feeling heard, valued, and respected. By embracing these principles, partners can create a harmonious and fulfilling partnership, regardless of the specific power dynamics they choose to adopt.

In exploring these ideas, it's enlightening to consider the perspectives of others who have examined similar dynamics. David Deida, for instance, delves into masculine and feminine dynamics, emphasising the importance of polarity in "The Way of the Superior Man." John Gray, in "Men Are from Mars, Women Are from Venus," explores differences in how men and women communicate, touching on how distinct roles can foster harmony. Esther Perel offers another intriguing perspective in "Mating in Captivity," examining how power balances affect intimacy and desire.

While these experts offer valuable insights, my approach centres on the idea that power dynamics should be as unique as the individuals involved. Whether one partner consistently leads or both share responsibilities, the arrangement should be rooted in mutual consent, respect, and adaptability. By integrating these principles, partners can craft a relationship that is both harmonious and fulfilling, accommodating the ever-changing nature of human connection.

Masculine and Feminine "Essence Polarity"

In modern society, the conversation around gender and its inherent roles continues to evolve and expand. Regardless of the gender assigned at birth, whether you were born male or female, I believe we all possess a blend of masculine and feminine essence or energy. Picture this spectrum: at one end lies the extreme masculine, and at the other, the extreme feminine. Using my circus analogy, this would be the Lion Tamer and the Lion. Between these two poles is a rich, dynamic blend of both energies, creating a unique tapestry for everyone.

Indeed, I find myself comfortably navigating this spectrum. I often tap into my masculine essence, yet I can seamlessly dial it down to embrace my feminine side when the situation calls for it. One moment, I might be deeply engaged in a lively discussion about football with the guys, and in the next, I could be chatting about

THE COACHING CORNER

parenting nuances with the girls. Does this make me the quintessential modern man? Not necessarily. I'm simply comfortable with who I am and appreciate the flexibility this blend offers. I take pleasure in my ability to transition between these energies, finding joy and fulfilment in both.

This balance, however, is not just a personal preference; it has practical implications in relationships. I finally discovered that I needed a partner who respected my dynamic, and I found someone whose essence complemented mine. While I enjoy leading our relationship, I do so with a partner who is both willing and equal; someone who desires to be led yet holds her own strength and autonomy. My ideal dynamic, which may not resonate with everyone, works perfectly for me, and that's not just acceptable; it's a wonderful breath of fresh air, and it flows.

Core Differences Between Masculine and Feminine Essence

Masculine and feminine energies each bring unique attributes and roles into relationships. The masculine essence is characterised by assertiveness, logic, protection, and focus, providing stability and direction through action and decisiveness. In contrast, the feminine essence embodies receptiveness, intuition, nurturing, and emotional awareness, fostering warmth and connection.

Key differences emerge in communication, with masculine energy being direct and goal-oriented, while feminine energy is expressive and emotive. For conflict resolution, the masculine favours logical and swift solutions, whereas the feminine values emotional processing and understanding. Intimacy for the masculine may centre around physical closeness, while the feminine seeks emotional connection. As for goals, the masculine is often driven by external achievements, while the feminine prioritises internal fulfilment and harmony.

Balancing these energies enriches relationships, promoting understanding and companionship. Embracing these differences can create a more fulfilling partnership, whether through "opposites attract" or harmonious similarities. The Circus Question helps you identify where you fall on this spectrum.

Inclusivity in the Spectrum

It's crucial to understand that the notion of masculine and feminine essence transcends traditional gender definitions. In other words, these energies are not confined to men being masculine and women being feminine. This spectrum is diverse and inclusive, making it applicable to all types of relationships, including homosexual partnerships. A same-sex couple can also embody this dynamic interplay of masculine and feminine energies, finding their unique balance and complementarity.

For instance, in a same-sex relationship, one partner might embody more masculine traits while the other leans into the feminine, or both partners might share these energies equally. The beauty of the polarity spectrum is its flexibility and inclusivity, allowing every individual and relationship to find its unique harmony.

THE COACHING CORNER
Historical Contexts and Shifting Roles

Historically, traditional relationship roles have often mirrored the extremes of this spectrum. For thousands of years, patriarchal systems have positioned the male as the head of the family, with the woman by his side; a model respected and perpetuated across many cultures, even today. This structure was deeply ingrained, with clear, distinct roles for each gender.

However, the 20th century brought monumental shifts, especially in Western cultures. The advent of the contraceptive pill, for instance, granted women unprecedented freedom. They were no longer confined to the roles of homemakers and mothers; instead, they could pursue careers and ambitions outside the domestic sphere. Motherhood could be postponed, and women could carve out identities independent of traditional expectations.

These changes have had profound implications for gender roles. Women have increasingly become providers, and in many single-parent families, they shoulder the responsibilities of both financial stability and security.

Men, too, have embraced more supportive roles within the home, with some even electing to be the stay-at-home parent. The notion of a man not being the primary breadwinner, once unthinkable, is now a viable option. This shift reflects a broader societal movement towards gender equality, yet it's not a one-size-fits-all solution.

As much as I champion gender equality, I've come to understand

THE COACHING CORNER

that it's a complex and nuanced issue. There are couples whose relationship dynamics diverge from this ideal of equality, yet they find harmony and fulfilment in their unique arrangements. Some may prefer traditional roles, while others thrive in more balanced or reversed roles. The beauty of our modern era is that there is space for all these variations.

Other authors and thinkers have also explored the interplay of masculine and feminine energies. For example, Carl Jung, the pioneering psychologist, introduced the concepts of the Anima and Animus. According to Jung, the Anima represents the feminine qualities within a man, while the Animus represents the masculine qualities within a woman. These archetypes are part of the collective unconscious and play a crucial role in shaping our personalities and behaviours.

David Deida, in his book "The Way of the Superior Man," discusses the importance of understanding and balancing these energies in relationships. Deida argues that a deep, intimate connection can be achieved when both partners embrace their inherent masculine or feminine essence while respecting the other's.

Interestingly, in "Beyond Mars and Venus," John Gray updates his ideas by acknowledging a shift in gender roles. He emphasises that both men and women now have both masculine and feminine qualities and that success in relationships requires balance and adaptability to navigate these evolving roles.

THE COACHING CORNER

The Circology System - The Perfect 10

All the circus roles can now be assessed in terms of a spectrum to reveal compatibility between them in real-world relationships; The Circology System is that methodology.

Imagine this spectrum not just as a linear scale but as a numerical system of polarity, where over 50 roles are numbered between 1 and 9. The higher the number, the more masculine essence, control, and leadership that role demands; conversely, the lower the number, the more feminine essence, less control, and more willingness to be led. Please refer to my Circology Polarity Spectrum Diagram.

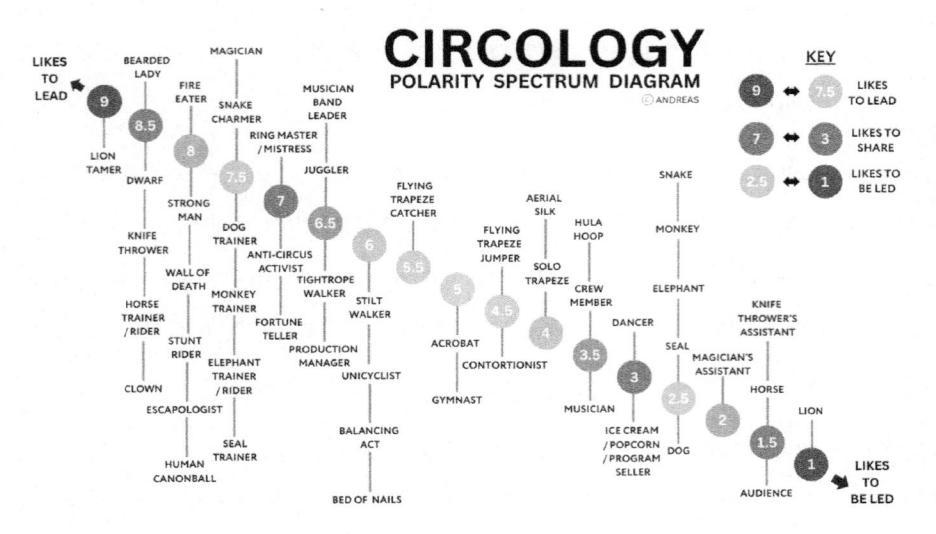

CIRCOLOGY POLARITY SPECTRUM DIAGRAM
© ANDREAS

KEY
- 9 ↔ 7.5 — LIKES TO LEAD
- 7 ↔ 3 — LIKES TO SHARE
- 2.5 ↔ 1 — LIKES TO BE LED

9 — LIKES TO LEAD: BEARDED LADY, MAGICIAN
8.5: FIRE EATER, MUSICIAN BAND LEADER
8: SNAKE CHARMER, RING MASTER / MISTRESS, LION TAMER, DWARF
7.5: JUGGLER, STRONG MAN
7: FLYING TRAPEZE CATCHER, KNIFE THROWER
6.5: DOG TRAINER, ANTI-CIRCUS ACTIVIST
6: WALL OF DEATH, TIGHTROPE WALKER, HORSE TRAINER / RIDER, MONKEY TRAINER, STILT WALKER, FLYING TRAPEZE JUMPER
5.5: STUNT RIDER, FORTUNE TELLER, ELEPHANT TRAINER, PRODUCTION MANAGER, UNICYCLIST, CLOWN, ACROBAT
5: ESCAPOLOGIST, AERIAL SILK, HULA HOOP, SOLO TRAPEZE
4.5: CREW MEMBER
4: SEAL TRAINER, HUMAN CANONBALL, BALANCING ACT, CONTORTIONIST, GYMNAST, DANCER
3.5: SEAL, MAGICIAN'S ASSISTANT
3: MUSICIAN, BED OF NAILS, MONKEY, ELEPHANT, KNIFE THROWER'S ASSISTANT
2.5: HORSE, ICE CREAM / POPCORN / PROGRAM SELLER
2: LION, DOG
1.5: AUDIENCE
1 — LIKES TO BE LED: SNAKE

Combining the scores, we seek the perfect 10. At the top end, you have partners who desire to lead, like the Lion Tamer (9), and at the bottom, those who prefer to be led, like the Lion (1), forging a perfectly imbalanced dynamic that works for them. In the middle,

THE COACHING CORNER

you find those seeking equality and shared responsibility, like the Flying Trapeze Flyer (4.5) and Catcher (5.5), aiming for a successfully balanced relationship. Just like the acts themselves, these roles are well-defined and work harmoniously for them.

Optimal compatibility is indicated by a score of 10, but the further away from 10, in either direction, the less compatible you may be. You may be overwhelmed or underwhelmed. By extreme example, two Lion Tamers (9) would have a score of 18, and although through similarities of character they may understand each other and become close friends, in a relationship, they're likely to compete and clash, leading to toxicity and potential failure. Conversely, two Lions (1), with a combined score of 2, would also struggle due to a lack of leadership, resulting in frustration and resentment.

Consider a Lion Tamer (9) dating a Solo Trapeze Artist (4), with a combined score of 13. The Lion Tamer's need for control conflicts with the Solo Trapeze Artist's desire for freedom and autonomy. This relationship could suffer from toxicity due to the Lion Tamer's frustration over a lack of control.

By utilising The Circus Question and The Circology System, you can identify compatibility with your ideal relationship partner. Embrace this tool to gain insight into your relationship dynamics and enhance your journey towards a fulfilling partnership. It's tried and tested; don't just take my word for it, test it for yourself and see. Ask potential partners the question playfully, exactly as it's written above. Do not explain why you're asking it, other than to pose it as an interesting question, and you're curious to know their answer.

THE COACHING CORNER

They may feel intimidated otherwise, and you need them to feel in a relaxed state for it to reveal their truth. Bear in mind their reluctance to answer it would be a red flag in itself!

By understanding and applying these principles, you can navigate the complexities of modern relationships with confidence and clarity. Explore The Circus Question through the Circology App or reach out via my website for personalized coaching and mentoring services. I primarily coach women, aiming to empower them to unlock the fullness of their relational potential, yet my system is designed to be beneficial to all. Let's embark on this transformative journey together and craft the love life you've always envisioned.

Seek the clarity and fulfillment in your romantic journey that you deserve. By exploring the unique insights offered through The Circus Question and Circology System, you can unravel the intricacies of compatibility and relationship dynamics. This method not only sharpens your self-awareness but also empowers you to make more informed choices in your dating life, ensuring you engage with partners who truly resonate with your values and aspirations.

Imagine a relationship that flourishes because both partners are attuned to each other's innate energies and strengths. Whether you're navigating the excitements of new connections or aiming to deepen an existing bond, the principles of Circology can guide you towards building a foundation that's both resilient and rewarding. The choice to understand and adapt to your and your partner's

THE COACHING CORNER

essence is a powerful step towards a harmonious, joyful partnership.

If you're ready to delve deeper into how these insights can transform your approach to relationships, consider downloading The Circus Question App or reaching out for tailored coaching support. My services are designed to offer guidance and clarity, especially for those eager to understand the nuanced dance of intimacy and connection. Through our collaboration, we can embark together on a journey towards meaningful, enriching relationships that celebrate who you are and what you truly need in a partner. Embrace the opportunity today to cultivate the love life that reflects the vibrant spectrum of your authentic self.

Indeed, the World of Love is a Circus!

Andreas

https://my.linkpod.site/Andreas_DatingCoach

THE COACHING CORNER

THE COACHING CORNER

Chapter 4

Total Freedom and Joy is your Birthright

By Linda Robinson

My Dream for You

Welcome to a journey of transformation! I'm **Linda Robinson,** and I want to share a dream that has fueled my life for the past 40 years—a dream where every individual awakens to their true selves, **embracing the total freedom and joy that is their birthright.** Imagine a world where everyone knows their worth, feels a deep sense of belonging, and experiences the love and connection we all crave.

As a transformational coach and workshop facilitator, I am dedicated to making this dream a reality. My mission is to help you discover your empowered magnificence, and guide you toward a life filled with passion, joy, and meaningful relationships. Having a

THE COACHING CORNER

career that feeds your soul and is in alignment with your purpose is not just for the lucky few. My passion is to help you dissolve the limiting beliefs that have you thinking that this is not possible; or that you don't deserve it. This is the Lie.

Please know you don't have to sacrifice or compromise who you are. Embracing your true self is your birthright, and you deserve to live authentically and fully. I dream of a world where people are just so happy to bring children into it. Because they know that the children are going to be treated with love, with respect, with honor, and growing up with these values and this interconnectedness of spirit and heart. And that everyone is going to know that total freedom and joy is theirs for the taking.

Of course, while the path to transformation is a journey, you don't have to take as long as I did. There are powerful tools and guidance available that can help you make quantum leaps.

My Heroic Journey

At 19 years old, I was working part-time in a company where all my coworkers hated their jobs and complained about not seeing their families enough, their children enough, and they couldn't wait for their 2-week vacation. This was a truly pivotal experience for me. It marked a turning point in my journey, because even at my young age, I felt deep down that life wasn't meant to be lived in sacrifice and without joy. My heart was breaking for them, but I didn't know how to tell them to make a change. I left the company after one month, moved from New York to California with my group of 8 friends, and opened a health food restaurant. But even more important than that, I began my quest on changing mindset, limiting beliefs, self fulfilling prophecies and patterned behavior.

I took a bit of a circuitous route through the exact opposites while I was seeking, learning and expanding my awareness. My journey took me through the despair of addiction, a divorce, disconnection from my family, and raising a daughter as a single mom at 23 years old. I had found myself deep in self-destruction and didn't know how to pull myself out. Still, I had this inner knowing that it didn't have to be that way and that all human beings were meant to live a quality life. That's *who* **I was, at my core, was whole and not broken.** I was fundamentally not any of these identifications or limitations. I came to understand that the beliefs, traumas, and coping mechanisms imposed on me had overshadowed my truest self—the one who is self-empowered and expansive, making healthy choices, and leading a life of quality and joy. But how would I find *her*?

I began seeking out every personal growth course, self-help study, meditation, Eastern and Western philosophy, and training I could find. I also embarked on a journey of recovery, and as I write this, I celebrate 32 years clean from all substances. The twelve-step programs talk about it being an "inside job"—healing the wreckage of our past and really coming to love ourselves. I suppose that the things that I did have contributed to that Self Love, appreciation, and acceptance of *all* of my life experiences. Many of my coaching clients say that the first thing they notice about me is how loving,

THE COACHING CORNER

caring and non-judgmental I am. They always feel safe to be themselves and share the hard conversations.

Testimonial

"Linda is a fantastic combination of heart and mind. She has a presence that unconditionally accepts me and whatever it is I'm going through while her intelligence dependably penetrates to the heart of the situation. She has been an extremely effective partner in helping me stay on purpose. With Linda's help, I have prospered financially while growing increasingly effective, resilient, centered, and, I have to say, joyful amid significant personal and professional challenges."

-John Utter... President, Thrive at Work

I am accepting of others because of the hell I lived through, feeling trapped in a lifestyle that was totally contrary to my beliefs and values. After healing the guilt and coming to terms with my own bad choices and actions, I know that every experience we go through is a vital thread in the tapestry of our lives, forming the unique quilt that represents each individual. Each experience is something to share with another; a lesson learned that can provide strength and guidance where needed. Not only in the recovery arena but in all situations that are disempowering and contrary to living our best life.

"Getting to the other side and dissolving the emotional charge and self judgments allows you to feel empowered and live from choice rather than patterned behavior." - Linda Robinson

THE COACHING CORNER

Exercise 1 – Limiting Belief Integration

Purpose: To integrate and dissolve limiting beliefs to live from your empowered choices

Start here for the best results:

1. Write down some of your limiting beliefs based on your challenges. (Some examples: I am not enough, I can't have it all, Money is scarce, Relationships are hard.)

2. Choose one of your limiting beliefs.

3. Relax, get quiet, and be present in the moment.

4. Feel this limiting belief fully and pay attention to what comes up (Examples: Images, Thoughts, Emotions, Body Sensations)

Begin the exercise:

1. Sit comfortably and be willing to go inside and follow the process to the best of your ability.

2. Choose the limiting belief(s) you want to work with.

3. Define its opposite. (Some examples: I am absolutely fabulous, having it all is my birthright, my life is filled with abundance, Relationships flow with ease and love.)

4. Feel the limiting belief. Make it strong and feel it fully. Verbally say something about it out loud or quietly. Take a deep breath in and out.

THE COACHING CORNER

5. Feel the opposite—the positive side. Feel it fully, magnify it and make it strong. Verbalize something about it out loud or quietly. Breathe deeply, in and out.

6. Repeat these steps 4 and 5 two more times, going back and forth between the opposing beliefs.

7. Then feel them both at the same time feeling each side simultaneously as you take a deep breath in and then slowly exhale. Verbalize what is happening between the two. Are they coming together? Do they still feel totally separate?

8. Repeat steps 4-7. Are they coming together more?

9. Imagine a ball of light above your head. Consciously draw in divine white light. Allow every cell in your body to soak it up as a sponge.

10. Integration:
    What are you more conscious of now than you were before?

    What was good about this for you?

    Do you feel like you have more choice in this area?

    What is one action you will take to ground this for yourself?

    What is your new narrative? Your new positive story around this belief.

Scan the QR code for a recorded demo of this process.

THE COACHING CORNER

Having it ALL in Relationship – Always Coming Back to Love

I was married to my husband Alex for 40 years before he passed away in 2017. Throughout our journey, we faced every challenge imaginable, even experiencing a period of separation. From those trials, **I gained invaluable wisdom** that helped us transform our relationship from dysfunction to one filled with love, connection, and fulfillment. We learned to communicate, listen, feel heard, and honored. We transformed our desire to be "right" or understood to prioritizing love and connection.

Do you ever feel attached to your position and opinion? Feel your partner just doesn't get you and they don't even listen? Does it escalate and break down the love and connection in the moment or even the whole day?

Here's what I learned:

- **You can't really communicate unless you are feeling the connection**

Each person wants to be heard and understood and vies for that space. "I won't get *you* until you hear and understand *me*". I finally asked myself, "What is more important—being right or the love between us?". I started saying to my husband, "Please, you go first. I want to understand you." I would grab his hand and listen and

THE COACHING CORNER

allow his perspective in. I would ask questions to really get where he was coming from. Once he had cleared his mind and felt received, he could hear me. We both adopted an attitude that we were on the same side, wanting to find a solution that was for the highest and best. Yes, sometimes there was compromise and one person got "their way" but we were at choice; not resenting the other or holding a grudge. Since we came from love compromise was easier and fairer in the long run.

- **Don't go to sleep mad or disconnected**

We wouldn't let any emotional charge or miscommunication stack up. It became important to make sure we completed each day clean with each other, feeling loving and connected. I realize this is easier said than done, but since you're reading this book, it's clear that you're eager to grow, empower yourself, and develop better strategies for a quality life.

- **Establish a Joint Mission**

What is the relationship's mission in the family, in the community, and in the world? My husband and I felt that we were helping to inspire others to make "love" the most important thing, to dissolve the "stack-ups" in their relationship and to connect to their hearts first. Through our journey, my daughter witnessed the possibility of change. She saw us transform from being argumentative and unhappy to becoming communicative and loving. During the last five years of my husband's life, he faced significant health challenges and was bedridden for the final two. I was determined

THE COACHING CORNER

to ensure he felt loved and never like a burden. When I felt drained, I reached out to my girlfriends and my Master Coach group for the support I needed, making sure to keep my energy positive. By the time he passed, we had shared everything that needed to be said. We had a deep understanding of the inspiration we brought to each other's lives and the honor it was to walk this path together.

- Have Lots of Fun Together

Ever heard of "date night"? How about "date weekend"? Make passion and love a priority otherwise you will end up roommates with no sizzle. Find things you like to do together. My husband and I liked to bicycle ride, and we loved to scuba dive. We took the most awesome vacations.

Exercise 2 – Cultivate Connection

It is important to feel connected *before* you communicate about the difficult topics and difference of opinion. Otherwise, you will not hear each other, and you will be more attached to being "right" than finding solutions together.

Scan the QR code below for a recorded demo of this process

That can help you feel heart and soul connected. It is a good exercise to do on a regular basis, but always do it before having challenging communications.

THE COACHING CORNER

Having it ALL: Prosperity, freedom and living a purpose filled life

Firstly, it is important to adopt the idea that you *can* have wealth, freedom, and a life that fills your soul. You may not know *how* yet but you must claim that identity for yourself. Somehow, I knew this inherently at 18 years old. Whatever we focus on expands. If we shift to this mindset more opportunities will come our way. If we believe we must settle, then that will be true.

I used to be a realtor, and I enjoyed it, but it wasn't my soul's calling. I made a list of my talents, abilities, and what made my soul sing. From that I realized that I loved helping people, making a real contribution to their lives, and seeing them live their dreams. I decided to be a coach. That did not mean that I knew how to create a coaching business that would support my lifestyle. Here is what I learned:

- Identify and dissolve limiting beliefs

Use the exercise on limiting beliefs in the earlier section. In the example I worked on "I don't know people who can pay what I am asking." and "It is spiritual work, and I shouldn't get paid."

The above are just two examples of my limiting beliefs. I did the processes and really came to know that Clients are Everywhere! I have conversations with people and see how I can help. The universe puts the right people in front of me. I also now know that it is fine to get paid for this kind of spiritual work. If I want to be a role model for what I teach, of course I can get paid well for my gifts and what I love to do. I am certainly serving others so it is natural there would be an exchange, and it aids accountability when there is "skin in the game".

- Money equals experiences

    It is easier to create money when I know what I want to do with it. The vacations I take, the legacy I want to leave for my daughter, the material things that are improving my quality of life, the philanthropy I give to good causes, and to others in need.

Exercise 3 – Write a list of 50 experiences you want to have

- Be specific and feel the emotions and how you will feel when you have it.
- Consider- How will it impact your life and those you care about?
- Create a vision board with photos, words and visuals that move you emotionally.

Exercise 4 – Visualize your Goals, Goal Activation

1. Make sure to have clear goals- write them down

Make them specific with a time deadline. Make sure you are connected to it emotionally. How will it impact your life?

2. Do this Slide Visualization Exercise:

Scan the QR code for a recorded guidance of this meditation.

THE COACHING CORNER

3. Don't Give Up!

    Don't ever give up when things get challenging? Sometimes we lose sight of the target. It's so important to stay connected to your "Biggest Why"! Especially if it is part of your purpose and your soul's calling, you *must* follow that inner inspiration. Remember that it happens in its own time. But if you keep the intention and do the processes, *It Will Happen.*

4. Be open to however it manifests

    When my husband was very ill, and I needed to care for him I didn't have the same energy for working or creating clients. I created a slide visualization that allowed for money to come into my life in any channel that flowed. I did not feel it had to come from my coaching business. Two unique things happened. First, a friend slipped a $14,000 check in her Christmas card to me. She wrote, "Dearest Linda, you have done so much for me in my life. I want to help you through this challenging time." I started crying with gratitude. Second, another friend introduced me to someone who taught me how to sell products on Amazon. I would never have thought of it, and it ended up netting me $50,000 in residual funds for 3 years straight.

THE COACHING CORNER

How can you be creative and open to financial flow?

Having It All

My life today is far beyond my wildest dreams. I am 72 years young at the time of this writing and I never felt more alive and vital. Every day I feel grateful and blessed. I have a career I love that fulfills me and feeds my soul. I help make a powerful difference in people's lives. I get to facilitate workshops with my daughter and that is very special to me. She is also a coach and an incredible human being. I have a boyfriend and we've been together 6 years. We have a passionate, loving relationship filled with mutual respect, excellent communication and great sex. I travel numerous times throughout the year to the most fabulous, exotic locations, scuba diving with my boyfriend, taking cruises with my brother, bonding with my daughter, and vacations with friends as a community. I love to box, exercise, play with my puppy and lie by my pool. I don't say this to brag but to inspire. All this is not just a chapter in my story; it's a continuous process, working on myself to defeat the self-sabotaging patterns and create life from an empowered place.

And you can get there too!

Be sincere and shift your mindset. Do the exercises. Focus on what you want to create. Don't focus on the negative or the past "failures". Focus on the "Wins" and your progress. Know you deserve it!

Ask yourself, "What would I need to do now to live, love and die complete and free without regret?" Live from that place now!

THE COACHING CORNER

Testimonial

I showed up for our scheduled appointment in tears. I was very shaken up and anxious about an altercation I had just had with my husband before walking out the door. This was in regard to a long-standing issue/point of friction between my husband and myself.

Within minutes of us beginning the process I felt calm and at peace. She guided me to a fresh perspective on the issue. The process was very spiritual in nature, and it immediately resonated with me on a deep level. With her guidance, I was able to get out of my small, restrictive frame of mind into a more expansive and loving place from which to view my "issue". From that expansive, heart centered place, I actually laughed at my "problem". I felt completely safe and secure in the knowledge that I was capable of dealing with it.

In addition to guiding me back to my spirit and heart center, she gave me some practical suggestions for how to approach my husband in our conversation about the topic. I was able to apply the lesson/approach that same day with outstanding results. My main fear was of the "confrontation" that I thought was coming with my husband. But after our session I felt no fear and no longer viewed it as a "confrontation" but as a process that I would work through in order to claim my power. I am SO grateful to have discovered Linda and this amazing way of processing difficult events! It was truly life altering.

Sincerely, Lisa P. RN, BSN

THE COACHING CORNER

"My greatest passion in life is seeing people awaken to who they are and to live that truth in their lives. The opportunity is to peel away everything that is not authentically you and allow the truth of you to emerge and blossom." - Linda Robinson

Contact Me

https://awakeningtotruth.com/

Linda@warriorsage.com

Free Discovery session: https://awakeningtotruth.com/discovery-session/

Scan the QR Code and let's book time together

We will look at your goals and dreams and investigate what is in the way. We will work on any challenge you are having. You will make progress in this Complimentary Experience.

THE COACHING CORNER

THE COACHING CORNER

Chapter 5

The Anatomy of Miracles:

Coaching And Training Medical Intuitives

By Skylar Acamesis

"Your Job is not to Seek for Health, Your Job is to Remove the Obstacles to it's already powerful presence within you." - Skylar Acamesis

The Beginning of a Silent Battle

At ten years old, I didn't know my life was about to split in two. One moment, I was a child like any other—racing my friends in the park, coming home with scuffed knees and sticky fingers. The next, I was trapped inside a body that felt like it was waging war against me. My parents had no roadmap for what came next. The doctors talked in clipped tones, their words heavy with diagnoses and vague reassurances. Autoimmune disease. Permanent. It took 3 years to get any diagnosis at all.

THE COACHING CORNER

I didn't understand the language of illness then, but I could feel its presence, creeping into every corner of my life. School became harder. Playtime turned into book time. My world narrowed as my body betrayed me. It wasn't just the physical symptoms; it was the isolation. What ten-year-old can explain why they can't run like they used to or why they're so tired all the time?

By the time I was 13, I realised the battle wasn't just against my body. It was against the expectations of a world that demanded productivity, energy, and perfection. I was failing their metrics. But something deep inside me screamed that there was more—more to life, more to healing, more to *me*.

I clung to that truth. It became my anchor on the days I could barely climb out of bed. It guided me through endless doctor visits and countless failed treatments. Even then, I felt that my story wouldn't end with suffering. That unrelenting truth planted a seed of power that would one day grow into something extraordinary.

The Breaking Point and the Breakthrough Point

When I was 19, my life imploded in the best way possible. I had reached my breaking point. The weight of years of illness, self-doubt, and the endless quest for answers had become too much to bear. I was tired of doctors telling me to manage symptoms meanwhile my pain was increasing and my youth slipping away. I was tired of feeling powerless. I was tired of masking symptoms. I was so done with pretending to be normal.

THE COACHING CORNER

One sleepless night, I found myself speaking to the sky, asking if there was a God for him to help me. That I couldn't do it alone. That life was just too hard. I didn't know it then, but I was on the edge of a spiritual awakening. Not the kind you read about in gentle meditations or self-help books—the kind that storms into your life, tears apart everything you thought you knew, and leaves you utterly transformed.

I stopped mid-step, overcome by a presence I couldn't name. It was as if the universe itself pressed pause and turned its full attention on me. The air shifted. My breath caught, and in that stillness, something deep and ancient made itself visible. I could see balls of light burning like the sun, and each sun contained an angel, each one singing, the sound stripped the defences of my soul and mind, and I fell to my knees sobbing as wave after wave of pain, shame and loneliness broke off my soul.

I didn't sleep that night. I didn't need to. A fire had been lit inside me—a fire that consumed every shred of doubt, fear, and hesitation. I threw myself into the study of healing, spirituality, and the connection between mind and body. As soon as I graduated law school I took off for London. I devoured ancient texts, modern science, and every resource I could find that spoke to the deeper truths of existence and started to run angel healing readings and healing events every Tuesday night.

For the first time, my illness didn't feel like a curse. It felt like a key—a way to unlock the hidden wisdom of the human body and soul. A way home to God. My intuition sharpened, my clairvoyance

THE COACHING CORNER

became a sword, and I began to see the world with a clarity I'd never known before.

This wasn't just about healing myself anymore. It was about understanding the profound connection between spirit, mind, and body—and discovering how we could reclaim the power to heal ourselves.

Birth of the Medical Intuitive Technique

The idea came slowly at first, like the first few notes of a song playing softly in the background. But over time, it grew louder, deeply insistent, demanding to be unleashed into the world.

What if healing wasn't about waging war on disease but finally hearing the law of truth our bodies have been tuned into and connected with all along? What if the power to heal wasn't hidden in a distant expert's hands or buried beneath the weight of treatments, but already woven into the fabric of who we are—waiting, longing to be unlocked?

This is the essence of the Medical Intuitive Technique, a groundbreaking discovery born from the understanding that true healing isn't about fixing what's broken—it's about remembering who we really are and tapping into unconditional health.

Through hypnosis, this technique powerfully guides the client back to God, back to the divine truth of their being, and back to themselves. It reaches into the depths of their soul to heal the original wound—the moment where pain first rooted itself and was given a false meaning, where the heart closed to protect what felt too tender to bear. The moment when we unknowingly came to subconsciously believe a lie.

But it doesn't stop there. The technique dismantles the spiritual and emotional strongholds that have convinced the body—so lovingly, so mistakenly—that illness is safer than health, and that pain is easier than freedom. These beliefs are not our enemies; they are the echoes of a body desperate to keep us safe in ways it learned long ago.

Imagine the power of standing in the sacred space where those illusions crumble, where the body finally understands it is free to heal, to thrive, to be whole. It's not a battle. It's a homecoming—a return to the truth of who we are.

But the journey of bringing the Medical Intuitive Technique into the world wasn't just spiritual—it was forged in the chaos of a pandemic. The trenches of COVID-19 became the crucible where this technique truly came alive.

As the world stood still, my healing clinic overflowed with requests. Hospitals shut their doors, cancelling surgeries and consultations. People who felt abandoned by traditional medicine began reaching out in desperation—not just my clients, but spiritual teachers, coaches, and healers themselves. They needed help not only for their clients but for their loved ones. They saw the results I was creating and asked me to teach what I had been practising for years.

THE COACHING CORNER

In the middle of this storm, I launched the first cohort of the Medical Intuitive Technique. Sixty-seven people joined the six-month programme, making it my first six-figure month. These weren't beginners—they were seasoned spiritual entrepreneurs and powerful healers. They didn't come to learn theory; they came to transform lives.

And transform they did. From the very first sessions, they began achieving results as profound as mine:

Results that Defy Logic:

Like A, who reversed stage 5 ovarian cancer in just 2 months.
Like B, who had her miracle baby after 4 heartbreaking miscarriages.
Like C, who healed her thyroid and reversed hair loss in just 3 weeks.
Like D, who successfully reversed her husband's brain tumour.

Imagine this: a collective quantum shift so profound that tears turn into laughter, creating a harmony of release and renewal. This is what happens when powerful, spiritually aligned entrepreneurs gather in a space designed for true growth—not just of our spiritual gifts, but of our very souls.

Today, there are over 150 practitioners using this technique worldwide. It's spreading not because of clever marketing or gimmicks but because it works. Each practitioner carries the torch, bringing this gift to their communities, their families, and their clients. Every session creates a ripple of healing that has no bounds, unlocking timelines of health and wholeness for people who thought they'd run out of hope.

This isn't just a technique; it's a revolution. A movement of souls committed to reclaiming the sacred art of healing. When you step into this work, you're not just learning a modality—you're stepping into a lineage of transformation, a legacy of miracles.

A New Era of Healing

We're living in a time of unparalleled transformation. The systems we once trusted—medicine, government, education—are being questioned like never before. Traditional medicine, while extraordinary in many ways, is limited by its focus on treating symptoms rather than addressing root causes. It places power in the hands of a select few, leaving patients disempowered and disconnected from their own bodies.

The Medical Intuitive Technique offers a revolutionary alternative. It dismantles the narrative that healing must come from external sources. Instead, it empowers individuals to step into their own power, to reconnect with the innate wisdom that has always been within them.

When I train practitioners, it's not just about teaching a technique. It's about igniting a movement. The people who come to me aren't novices. They're already leaders—spiritual teachers, six- and seven-figure entrepreneurs, and healers transforming lives in their own right. But they come because they know there's a deeper level of transformation waiting for them.

THE COACHING CORNER

They don't just learn to heal others—they heal themselves in ways they never imagined possible. Every breakthrough, every revelation, every session is a testament to the limitless potential we all carry.

This is not just healing; it's liberation.

The Problems That Keep You Awake at Night

If you're reading this, I know you've felt it too. That gnawing sense that there's something more waiting for you. Maybe you're a coach or a healer, already doing incredible work, but you feel like you're scratching the surface of what's possible. You're ready to go deeper but don't know how.

Maybe your clients aren't getting the results you know they're capable of. You're frustrated by the blocks you can't seem to shift, the patterns that refuse to budge. Or maybe it's personal. Maybe you're carrying your own wounds—old traumas, chronic pain, or a sense of emptiness that no amount of success can fill.

I see you. I've been you. And I want you to know this: the answers you're seeking aren't out there. They've been within you all along. The "Medical Intuitive Technique" isn't just a tool—it's the key to unlocking the power you've always had. It's the bridge between where you are and where you're meant to be.

Returning Power to Humanity

This isn't just a technique. It's a revolution. A reclamation of the power that has always belonged to us but has been systematically

THE COACHING CORNER

stripped away by a world that paradoxically profits from our disease and disconnection. Imagine a world where healing isn't a privilege but a birthright. Where people no longer live at the mercy of their bodies or their pasts. Where we don't just treat symptoms but eradicate the root causes of suffering—physical, emotional, and spiritual. This is the vision driving the Medical Intuitive Technique. It's not just about healing individuals—it's about healing humanity. It's about creating unconditional health. The world is changing faster than any of us can fully comprehend. Old systems are crumbling, and new possibilities are emerging. This is your invitation to be part of that change. To step into your power. To become a leader in this new paradigm. You don't have to do it alone. The path is already here, waiting for you. All you have to do is reach out. I got you.

Connect with me:

Medical Intuitive Association

Instagram: /skyacamesisInstagram: @skylaracamesis

Twitter: @skyacamesis

YouTube: /c/Skylar444

Telegram: https://t.me/+iQGzpg4NIOw0MTNk

Linktree: https://linktr.ee/skylaracamesis

THE COACHING CORNER

THE COACHING CORNER

Chapter 6

Wisdom Coaching

By Dr Suzanne Henwood

Does Coaching Over Promise?

What is your experience of coaching? Is it something you feel is of value? Is it a quick fix? Or is it only for elite leaders? Or is it bordering on therapy and way too scary?

In my experience the reality is – It depends!

Coaching has shown me life can be messy and complex. And I want to share with you a new approach to coaching I am creating and how I applied it in a real-life scenario.

I am on a journey of exploration about what coaching is, what it isn't and what it can be. I have been reflecting on claims around 'quick fixes' or 'magic bullets' and it has got me curious as to

THE COACHING CORNER

whether coaching truly gives people the ability to tackle complexity and systemic change in today's world. In particular, does it encourage people to go beyond themselves?

Let me tell you about my journey, as a coach and a coaching client, and how I have grown personally and professionally through challenging my own perception of what coaching is.

My Story

I have been a coach for 25 years. I am qualified in a number of modalities and I am a multi award winning Neuroscience Based Coach. I am an Amazon best-selling author (since October 2024) and a researcher in the field. You might think then that I have got my own life completely sorted. But you would be wrong! I still benefit hugely from coaching. I have successes and failures, great connections and troubling conflicts – I live a real life. I benefit from getting professional support and I am OK tapping into wisdom beyond me. In fact, I cannot imagine life without doing that.

A New Approach

I stopped expecting myself to have all the answers a long time ago. I've also learned to let go of beliefs like "I'm broken" or "I am inadequate". The truth is, life is complex and ever-changing, and it's impossible to navigate it alone. This is why I've developed a new coaching approach that provides both myself and my clients with the support we need to genuinely meet our challenges and achieve our goals.

THE COACHING CORNER

As I started to research and learn about the modern world, as well as tapping into ancient spiritual traditions and the multiple sources of wisdom and intelligence, I started to get really excited. I started to consider a new model of wholeness: within myself, outside of and beyond myself and between myself and other people and the world around me. And the realisation that it is all available to me right here, right now, if I know how to tap into it. This is changing my philosophy of coaching, and quite frankly changing my life.

I ask myself questions like:

- What if it is not about having more, being more, doing more – but rather reclaiming what already is?
- What if we stopped fighting ourselves and each other and artfully guided real wisdom to emerge?
- What if by connecting to, and tapping into, the multiple intelligences that define the systemic nature of our humanness, we can tap into a place where change emerges naturally and in alignment within, without and between?
- What if we coached to (and from) this place of deep connection; within the body, mind, heart and soul, and without through community and collaboration, so that a new level of wise being can arise.

I began to explore accessing this systemic, integrated wisdom intelligence, and as I did all sorts of new things started to open up: new possibilities, deeper change, sustainable change,

THE COACHING CORNER

allowing you to live life fully and truly being all you were created to be.

As I explored this in my own life, it felt like coming home to myself. I found a safe place to be and to belong. And, I didn't have to sell my soul to find that elusive happiness I had been chasing that always felt like it was controlled by someone else – or someone else's system. Now I was plugged back into the multiple interrelated wisdom sources.

Systemic, Integrated, Embodied, Multiple Intelligences – iWisdom Coaching

iWisdom Coaching is a new model of coaching I am creating, that helps clients to love themself back to wholeness. It is about accessing a deep and real integrated wisdom within, without and between, that enables you to be fully and authentically yourself – and for that to be more than enough.

The coaching approach is as unique as you are. As a coach my role shifts to creating an integrated sacred space for clients, that works systemically, contextually and dynamically, to enable both our own unique, and collective wisdom to emerge, that is perfectly right for that client, at that moment in time. by:

- deepening consciousness
- breaking unresourceful patterns
- increasing impact in the world
- (re)connecting with self, others and the world

- equipping and supporting clients to be wholly aligned with who they are
- understanding their unique contribution and purpose in the world
- finding and fully accessing their vitality and power
- embracing the concept of human becoming
- giving permission for your human spirit to come alive
- opening and shifting world views
- accepting fully and loving who they are
- and contributing to the health and sustainability of the world

This is a form of Transformational Wisdom Intelligence to become truly human.

iWisdom Coaching Model

The iWisdom Coaching Model works across 12 Intelligence Arenas:

> **Internally:** Head, Heart, Gut, Pelvis and Autonomic Nervous System and Somatic Body, using Breathing as a key access point.

> **Externally:** Environment, Social/Interpersonal, Technological, Trauma/ Safety, Spiritual, Quantum

The systemic and integrated approach of iWisdom Coaching focuses on the multiple intelligence arenas and the interconnectedness between them. Using a heuristic framework, iWisdom Coaching works to create coherence and alignment

THE COACHING CORNER

across these centres of intelligence, guided by a philosophy of wise compassion. This enables each intelligence to function at its wisest expression. By elevating the client's global systemic awareness, their internal wisdom is further enhanced, fostering a deeper sense of clarity and insight."

While the process can begin anywhere in the system, often the level of consciousness initially is greatest within, so the coach initially guides the client to a high degree of self-awareness, including any intelligence preferences, or blocking (within or between the different intelligences).

Recognizing that no individual exists in isolation, the coach expands the focus to include the broader system—encompassing interpersonal relationships, social connections, and the surrounding environment, including technology and AI. This approach considers key concepts such as global shifts, ecology, patterns, collective wisdom, and spiritual philosophy.

Given the systemic and dynamic nature of the 12 interconnected components, the coach continuously reassesses shifts both within the individual and across the wider system. This process acknowledges that any change in one area of intelligence will ripple throughout the entire system, influencing all other components."

Exploring this in Context

Let's apply this to a real-life situation, allowing you to reflect on how it enhances awareness and consciousness—elements that may be overlooked in more traditional coaching approaches."

Case History

The client is myself, as that gives the best possible history and context from my perspective, while eliminating any concern around confidentiality. Some details are changed, to avoid naming other parties involved.

I sought coaching intermittently from 2019 to 2024.

In 2019, I lost a great mentor, a dear friend, and teacher after a brief illness - Grant Soosalu. For the two to three years leading up to his death, I had supported him in various ways: writing jointly authored articles that he reviewed before submission, delivering courses on his behalf, and meeting with him in the final weeks of his life. He thanked me for being a co-creator of the field. During the last meeting he entrusted me with the responsibility of "looking after his baby - mBraining" - a coaching modality he had originally created with Marvin Oka.

His death was a profound loss, and my grief was difficult to express as I tried to support others while stepping into the roles he had asked me to take on. All of this unfolded while I was also managing my own business and navigating the challenges of the new position, dealing with a small group of individuals who sought to take control for themselves.

THE COACHING CORNER

In November 2019, about 5 months after his passing, I was rushed to the hospital and diagnosed with a minor stroke and a cardiac issue. I spent a week in a cardiac ward. My sense was that the combination of unprocessed grief and a sense of betrayal from those I had trusted, had triggered an autonomic dysregulation in my body.

Although I leaned on my skills in wellbeing coaching to recover physically, the deeper emotional and relational issues lingered. Finally, in 2024, I made the difficult decision to relinquish my licenses in the modality my mentor had asked me to lead as I could see no way forward and it was clear some people wanted me out of the way. Inside my head my inner voice was asking: *Had I failed? Could I have done more? Were the coaching tools I taught not as effective as we had claimed? How could this be happening?*

The reality was that this was a complex, systemic issue that extended far beyond me personally.

Throughout this time, I sought various forms of coaching and therapeutic approaches, including Havening (a psychosensory touch technique), TRE (Trauma Release Exercises), ACT (Acceptance and Commitment Therapy), NLP (Neuro-Linguistic Programming), and mBraining, among others. Despite my efforts, my nervous system remained frequently dysregulated, sleep was elusive, my heart felt heavy with sorrow, my gut was in turmoil, and several physiological indicators remained outside of normal range. I could not bring my body back into coherence, something that had once come relatively easily to me.

No matter how much I tried, I couldn't seem to "let go" or move forward. There was an unresolved injustice, 'unfinished business' and a lingering hope that somehow, in time, I could find a positive way through. I felt diminished by the entire experience.

As I reflect on the iWisdom Coaching Model, I invite you to consider: What might you be curious about across the 12 intelligence arenas?

Take a moment to note your thoughts on each arena. What would you want to explore more deeply? Where do you feel the heaviest burdens might lie, and how would you approach addressing them?

Inner	
Head	My head has retold the story over and over to try to gain understanding (and we know that can create issues with accuracy, negative neuroplasticity).My head took time to find evidence, documentation and recordings to check out my perceived accuracy. Through coaching I have explored any meanings I have attached to events, which may be linked to previous history, and safely challenged those.

THE COACHING CORNER

Heart	My heart was devastated, at the loss of my mentor and friend, and at the betrayal from others in the community. So much so that I was hospitalized with a stroke and ECG changes and I am now on cardiac medication for life as a daily reminder of that.
Some connections fell away, I was 'unfriended' on social media by the small group involved and I was excluded from the very community I had been asked to lead. Being the "only one he trusted" (his words) felt a lifetime away, as I was gaslit and ghosted by those I had trained, equipped and supported. The injustice stabbed me deep in my heart.
Key values that were transgressed for me included: honesty, integrity, loyalty and trust.
Gut	My gut, having done years of self-development work, had a solid grounded base of identity to stand on. Yes, of course I checked out my own behaviours, and no I did not always remain calm, regulated and truly compassionate towards the perpetrators, but I had a good sense of

THE COACHING CORNER

	who I was and my intentions, which probably provided enough stability to keep going. There were boundaries that had been transgressed that needed re-evaluating and at times I felt unsafe, with no voice. My business was under threat; my reputation at risk; and some of my 'tribe' connections were lost, threatening my sense of belonging. The situation was inescapable, a sure indication of trauma.
Pelvis	I had been asked to look after the "baby". I felt it was not possible to just walk away as I would have been walking away from the vision I had aligned to and dedicated myself to for over 10 years and I would be letting down my mentor. I wanted to nurture and protect the 'baby'. The alignment with the vision, and the deep connection to pelvis, stopped me walking away quickly, which impacted my health over time. My drive and energy diminished as my role was challenged, and my place in the field faded. It was a deep grief and loss. As I spent time with my mentor before he died, I

THE COACHING CORNER

	was reminded that he said "You laugh a lot". But I had stopped laughing. My sense of purpose was being challenged. I had committed my whole self to the field and other people wanted me gone.
Autonomic Nervous System (ANS)	I believe it was a dysregulation of my autonomic nervous system which meant I ended up in a cardiac ward. An existential threat to my whole being. I was unable to get into physiological coherence (which I had previously been able to do very easily), I could not regulate my body temperature (an ANS function), and I was living life in a constant mild to moderate sympathetic reaction, which I struggled to get myself out of. Upon discharge from hospital, I had to work hard to get my confidence back. Even leaving the house on my own initially was too hard, for fear of another health event. On many levels I did not feel safe to exist.
Somatic Body	My heart reacted so badly, I was tested for a heart attack and kept in a cardiac unit for a week and placed on medication for life.

THE COACHING CORNER

	I was diagnosed with a minor stroke, which initially left me struggling to access words and slightly disorientated in terms of time and understanding of events. As a trainer and speaker this created an existential threat to my purpose of being a coach, speaker and trainer.
Breathing	Through knowledge of a variety of breathing techniques, I used breathing throughout, which I am sure reduced how much I was impacted physiologically.
Outer	
Environment – locally	My environment locally shrunk in the first instance as I was disconnected from my tribe. And personally, I reduced my social connections to key support people, with whom I could feel safe.
Environment – Globally	Support from core friendships and family members came largely through social media, which gave regular safe contact as I found my way back to a new normality. The global betrayal was ongoing and had a huge impact on many aspects of me and my business. I watched a new narrative unfold which just wrote me out of the story.

THE COACHING CORNER

Technology	Technology played a mixed role: with positive educational opportunities, social connections and staying in touch with the world; while also making disconnection evident and gave some people access to me at a vulnerable time, who I would have preferred to be distant from.
Trauma / Safety	Beyond the aspect of safety already mentioned, the ongoing issues of betrayal, were, I believe, a large part of the reason I took time to recover. A previous bullying incident at an academic workplace was also triggered, which led me to do some trauma work and release on the combination of both events.
Spiritual	My faith was another solid rock which gave me groundedness and support throughout. The sense of there being someone beyond me, overseeing what was happening and the calmness that prayer brought – was like a form of meditation with God. The ability to trust that God had a bigger picture than I was aware of in that moment, helped me put the events in some perspective, opening a gateway to the future again.

THE COACHING CORNER

Quantum	It was evident to me that the behaviours of a small group of people was a huge contributor here. The unique role of the field of coaching in moving the paradigm of coaching forward, was, in my view being challenged. I was left questioning that bigger picture. Was this a space I wanted to be in moving forward?

My desired outcome from coaching was to:

- Have a safe place to explore the whole system and raise my levels of consciousness around it from multiple perspectives
- To find some clarity about my role and to make wise decisions moving forward
- To disrupt unresourceful neural pathways in me that were causing reactions that were not helpful
- To regulate my system to reduce the stress response and regain balance and coherence
- To heal the damage already done in my body

What is clear to me is that a talking, head-based style of coaching would not have got to the core of the issues. A new more encompassing model was required to handle the complexity of today's world. I wanted a model that was dynamic, integrated and systemic, to raise consciousness and reach into the beyond me / we / collective realm. The need to both enhance

THE COACHING CORNER

self-awareness and to refocus on more than I – to look at service, contribution, meaning, purpose and legacy has never been more timely.

As I created the iWisdom model I was excited that what was emerging was a way to help people to explore and create a version of themselves that is beyond being – to becoming in a complex and fast changing world. To create a wiser form of best evolving self – while fully embracing and accepting the here and now.

In Summary

Coaching has evolved significantly since the term "coach" was first used at Oxford University in 1830, and it continues to adapt in response to the changing needs of our world. The boundaries between coaching, counselling, therapy, and mentorship are increasingly fluid, creating a unique opportunity to build a dynamic, modern coaching practice that embraces wholeness.

iWisdom Coaching is an integrated, neuroscience-based coaching approach, grounded in research and proven professional practice. It offers a systemic coaching model that encompasses 12 distinct intelligences, providing a comprehensive framework for transformation.

As humans, we are complex, ever-evolving systems, constantly responding to the world around us. Our thoughts, emotions, and behaviours shape how we live our lives—and, in turn, influence those around us and the world we inhabit. While many coaching

THE COACHING CORNER

models focus on a single dimension of human experience, iWisdom Coaching recognizes the need for a more holistic approach. Talk-based coaching can help clarify thinking and planning. Somatic coaching connects us to the wisdom of the body. Psychosensory touch techniques harness the power of touch to rewire neural pathways. Each of these approaches offers valuable insights, but alone, they may not fully address the complexity of human experience.

Over the past 25 years, I have trained in a wide range of coaching, counselling, and therapeutic methods, and have integrated these into a cohesive, modern approach. *iWisdom Coaching* brings together the most effective tools, tailored to meet the unique needs of each client within a global, systemic context. This integrated methodology honours the individuality of each person while considering the interconnectedness of all systems.

iWisdom Coaching provides a new path for both aspiring and experienced coaches—an approach that fosters personal and professional excellence. It offers a competitive edge for those seeking to deepen their coaching practice and make a lasting impact in the field.

If you would like to know more – reach out to me through social media:

Linktree: https://linktr.ee/drsuzannehenwood

It would be my pleasure to support you.

THE COACHING CORNER

Scan The QR Code

THE COACHING CORNER

Chapter 7

The Art of Living Fierce

By Ian Norton

From Prison to Princess – The Journey to Fierce Self-Confidence

What do I say when people ask me why I think I can help them? I'll be honest, I'm 63, I've been around a long time. I am a flawed individual like anyone else. No one's perfect, right? But let me tell you how I got from where I was to where I am, and hopefully, you will see why I am passionate about helping other people with their journey to Fierce Self- Confidence.

Firstly, when I was young, I knew I was capable of something great. I was intelligent, intuitive, and creative, but I was also deeply insecure, lacked self-confidence and I was a relentless people pleaser. This led to some bad mistakes, some ...very... bad....

THE COACHING CORNER

mistakes. One of these people pleasing ended me in Wandsworth Prison for 4 months.

After that, life was shall we say challenging? But what I learned was that with the right mindset and the correct strategies and beliefs, you can achieve anything! I investigated coaching, trained with Tony Robbins, studied NLP (neuro linguistic programming) studied to be a counsellor, trained as an actor, a hairdresser, an image consultant, an etiquette, and protocol expert, eventually having the opportunity to work with Princess Diana on etiquette and personal self-confidence. Ask me about it another time.

Added to this, I have gone through a lot. I grew up in a very male dominated family, as such, being GAY (oh, did I mention, I'm gay?) was not an option. I had to hide who I was and pretend to be someone I wasn't. I married a woman because that was what was expected. The guilt, the anxiety, the shame, often made me consider suicide as the "easy option."

After 20 years of marriage, I couldn't do it anymore, I came out. I lost my wife, my home, many friends, and my dog! I met a man who loves me, and we have been married for 12 years. Fairytale, eh? Not really...

In the past few years, my father died from a stroke, my brother died unexpectedly at 63, my best friend died 3 months later, a week before her 40th birthday. My mother who had advanced dementia died after 8 years of care. So, I have experienced depression, guilt, dementia, anxiety, bereavement, coming out, divorce, loss of identity, direction, the list goes on...

I don't tell you this for sympathy, just to let you know that when we work together, and I say I understand- I REALLY understand.

Today, I am proof that your past does not define your future. I've taken every lesson, every hardship, and every setback to build a life I'm proud of. My journey from prison to princess has been unconventional, but it's mine, and I embrace it fully.

Now, I'm a personal development coach- focused on transforming your personal and professional presence. It's not just coaching- I combine life coaching, etiquette expertise, business strategy, and image consulting to help my clients make a lasting impact—whether you're stepping into a boardroom, networking, or just want to feel more confident in your everyday life. I work with professionals, executives, and entrepreneurs, anyone who feels their potential doesn't fully show in how they present themselves and are ready for a complete transformation. If you're looking to lead with confidence, enhance your presence, and align your outward image with your inner goals, let's talk. My aim is not to change you, but to guide you to find yourself and discover your own FIERCE SELF CONFIDENCE.

From Stuck to Supercharged

As you can see, my path to becoming a coach was big on self-discovery and transformation. I knew that true confidence wasn't just about "feeling good"—it was about finding clarity, purpose,

THE COACHING CORNER

and belief in my abilities. This could only come from proof, from results – in short confidence can only come retrospectively.

Imagine this for a moment: You are in a room full of people, but you feel invisible. You're pushing yourself hard at work, but no one seems to notice your effort. You're in a relationship, but you feel lost or that it should be so much more. You wonder if you're truly worthy of the love or success you desire. Doubts are constantly in your head and no matter how much you try to keep up appearances, inside, you feel "not enough"—like something is missing. You're not alone in this feeling, and it's exactly why I help people transform. When it's time to shift from self-doubt to fierce self-confidence, from feeling unseen to feeling unstoppable, I am there to support you.

Through years of personal work, professional training, and an obsession to understand the psychology of confidence and self-image, I created my unique coaching style, an approach that goes beyond traditional coaching. I developed tools, methods, and strategies that allow you to fully embrace your potential and live with total self-belief, fierce self-confidence, and magical presence. Today, I am honoured to mentor and coach others along this path, helping them find their unique strengths, build resilience, and unlock the self-assuredness they need to become both the person they want to be and the person they want others to see.

Working with me isn't just about motivation; it's about complete and sustainable transformation. Motivation comes and goes. Consistency and repetition last. My clients don't just feel supported—they feel empowered, prepared to handle challenges, and ready to make lasting changes. They are FIERCE! Together, we break down anything holding them back, removing blocks, making over their self-image and giving them a way forward that's as bold and limitless as their dreams. (by the way, we get those dreams, goals and visions in crystal clear shape too!)

Mirror, Mirror: The Bold Truth About Inner Confidence and Outer Power

In today's image-obsessed society, people often focus on "looking" confident rather than "being" confident. Hiding behind, make-up, hair extensions, and an expensive suit, rather than enhancing what they have because they are proud of themselves. It's easy to think that confidence comes from perfecting our appearance or putting on a brave face. But in my work, I teach a different truth: true confidence doesn't come from appearance alone; it radiates from within. Don't get me wrong, the outside matters, which is where my styling, fashion and image knowledge comes in. But how we present ourselves is as much about how we feel as it is about how others view us.

When clients arrive feeling "not enough," they're often experiencing a disconnect between their inner self and how they present themselves to the world. Many feel trapped in the cycle of insecurity, doubt, feeling unseen, feeling judged, questioning their self-worth and in turn struggling to project who they really are. I recently had a client, Jane, who had been promoted at work. She

THE COACHING CORNER

now had to present at Boardroom meetings and liaise with C-Suite level executives. Despite clearly being capable (she was invited to take the job, she didn't even have to apply for it) she felt she wasn't good enough, wouldn't be taken seriously, and felt she was "not enough". After a few months of working together, she is not only acing her presentations, she has in the last month landed an account that she has been chasing for over a year but didn't feel she was good enough to land. Go her! You see, I work with clients to break down these kinds of mental blocks, helping them connect with their core values and recognise all the unique strengths they bring to the world.

With this energised self-awareness, my clients no longer feel pressured to "fake it". They can strut their stuff as their true selves, grounded in a confidence that is real and lasting. This internal shift creates an outer presence that's powerful and magnetic, drawing people in and creating opportunities that reflect their true self-worth.

Imagine the feeling of stepping into any room, any meeting, or into any situation without anxiety or self-doubt, knowing you are a force to be reckoned with, a warrior, a sovereign, a magnetic superstar. Eyes are on you because you exude energy, confidence, and style. This is what my clients achieve—an alignment of their inner and outer selves that makes them feel UNSTOPPABLE. They no longer ask themselves, "Am I enough?" They are showing up with the presence, resilience, and integrity that tells the world, "I'm here, and I am fierce."

THE COACHING CORNER

Why People Seek Me: Fierce Confidence, Real Results

When clients come to me, they're not just looking for a quick fix; they're ready to make big changes. Often there has been a major event – a career change, a relationship breakdown, a bereavement, something that has finally made them feel that the pain of staying as they are, will be worse than the discomfort of change. They've often spent years struggling with all those nagging blocks that keep them from taking a chance or making a change, leaving that toxic relationship, and going after a dream career. They are tired of living with self-doubt, anxiety, or the constant feeling of being unseen and unnoticed. They want clarity, purpose, and a sense of self that feels true to them.to feel they can have, be and do all they are worthy of.

My unique approach offers a formula for addressing these barriers and creating real, transformation inside and out. Together, we focus on five key areas:

Clarity: We dive deep into clients' values, beliefs, and goals to help them uncover their genuine desires, not what they think they should want or what others want. Many people feel "stuck" because they're not clear on what they truly want or need, the focus on what they don't want. This means they are still looking at the negatives. Example – If I say now, don't think about an elephant...what are you now thinking about? See, by saying "I don't want this, I don't want that," we still focus on it. This is why what you DO want is so important. Through simple exercises, I help

THE COACHING CORNER

clients gain clarity on their purpose and vision, creating a blueprint that matches who they are at their core.

Confidence: As I've mentioned, confidence isn't something we're born with; it's a skill we can build, a feeling or emotion we can learn to create instantly. Through my specialised strategies, I help clients develop the confidence to go after their goals and embrace challenges rather than shy away from them. By working through any fears, limiting beliefs, and past experiences, or childhood traumas, we build a solid base of self-trust that empowers my clients to take action, make decisions, and truly see themselves for the amazing people they are.

Resilience: Life is full of difficulties, things go wrong, sh** happens. It's easy to be all positive and motivated when things are going great, but what about when the unexpected happens? Resilience is the key to navigating those situations rather than defaulting to old bad habits. So, I teach my clients practical resilience-building techniques, from handling setbacks to coping with rejection, transcending difficult and negative emotions to handling overwhelm. They learn how to bounce back from challenges with a renewed sense of strength and determination.

Connection: For me connection is the most important skill we can have. Many clients struggle to communicate confidently, especially in situations where they feel vulnerable. They misread others, or place wrong meanings on what's said or written. We all come at a situation from our own experiences and perspective after all. I work with people to develop communication skills that allow them to express themselves clearly and honestly and to see beyond the obvious in others. They learn to show up fully, creating a presence that's both powerful and relatable. The skills include body language, empathy, connection, mirroring, and active listening. These skills will be with you for life.

Self-Image: Transformation is a journey, not a destination. I guide clients in developing a sustainable self-care practice that supports their journey. They learn how to prioritise their mental and emotional well-being. How to place importance on themselves and to prioritise their needs rather than leaving it till everything else is taken care of. As I often say, you can't give what you haven't got. We explore nonverbal, and physical communication, basically, we check out your personal style, hair, make-up, business or personal dress. We can do a wardrobe edit, lose your comfort zone mentality and upgrade you to the new "YOU 2.0".

We look at how you present yourself, including many of the techniques I shared with Princess Diana. We look at where you may be struggling – interviews, office, socially, school gates, wherever you find yourself less than fierce, we tackle it head on. This creates a skillset that allows you to thrive in all areas of your life.

By tackling these areas, clients experience a "total self-reset." They move from feeling anxious, unseen, or unsure to exuding a presence that's magnetic, self-assured, and one that truly reflects who they are and how they want to be seen. I had a client, a single mum with a 2-year-old and a newborn. Dad had substance abuse issues and was no longer in the picture. This client came to me

THE COACHING CORNER

because her local paper had done an article about women at the school gates in their pyjamas. She had been featured in some of the images and felt a complete failure. In a brief time, I helped her realise that dealing with all she had gone through and managing two young children was a huge deal and she began to give herself some credit. By the way, she was in joggers and a hoodie, not pyjamas! Who wouldn't be? Anyway, we worked on her self-love and did some shopping for a couple of outfits for when she could actually go out with her friends. We changed the way she felt about her situation, and we changed what she did about her situation. It is still difficult for her, but she feels in control, empowered, no longer a victim, and no longer judged.

What I coach isn't just about short-term improvements; it's a lifelong transformation. I'll also add that nothing can surprise me. I had a call once from the Sultan of Brunei's people who wanted me to sort out his helicopter pilot's personal hygiene! I've personally shopped with Joan Collins, styled for Vivienne Westwood, I have a lovely client who was a personal trainer, spent all her time dashing from gym to gym and felt she wasn't a businesswoman but wanted to change her life. Clearly as a self-employed personal trainer she WAS a businesswoman, but not in her head. 18 months on from starting work with her, she now has her own Wellbeing Centre which has a gym but also offers reiki, Indian head massage and other holistic treatments.

All things are possible with the right amount of self-belief.

THE COACHING CORNER

No Nonsense, All Impact: Coaching Approach

How do we achieve this? When people work with me, they don't just get a series of exercises or vague advice I read in a book. There is no "one size fits all" approach. You get transformative, actionable guidance that leads to real change. My coaching approach which I've honed over many, many years is caring and understanding, but it's also direct and no BS. I'm here to guide you in owning the challenges and developing the tools you need to build a life that's quite frankly, bloody awesome.

My coaching includes:

Visualisation Exercises: You learn to create a mental image of your ideal self, envisioning your best life in vivid detail. This helps you clarify your goals, overcome any limiting beliefs, and build a sense of possibilities.

Mindfulness and Grounding Practices: I teach clients mindfulness techniques to calm their mind, reduce anxiety, and build mental resilience. This allows you to approach challenges with clarity and focus, staying grounded in moments of stress or uncertainty.

Confidence-Building Frameworks: We work on developing a confidence mindset that's based on resilience and self-assuredness. You will be certain you can handle anything and be fine with the outcome. Clients learn to handle criticism, navigate setbacks, and pursue their goals with courage and commitment.

Goal Setting and Action Planning: Together, we create inspiring

THE COACHING CORNER

goals that align with your vision. Each goal is broken down into manageable steps, providing a clear path forward.

Personalised Feedback and Support: Throughout the coaching process, I provide ongoing feedback and support, helping you stay accountable and make progress. You receive guidance tailored to your specific needs, ensuring that every step you take brings you closer to your dream outcome.

My clients experience real, lasting change through this approach. They walk away from each session with practical tools, a sense of empowerment, and a renewed confidence in their ability to create a life that excites them. When they look in the mirror, they love who is looking back.

Living Fierce: From Quiet Dreams to an Unforgettable Life

The ultimate goal of my work is to empower clients to live fully, boldly, and beautifully. When you work with me, I want you to be equipped to live what I call the "Live Fierce life"—a life that's fierce, fearless, purposeful, glamorous and deeply fulfilling. This transformation isn't just about feeling more confident; it's about being more confident, being resilient, and being real.

Imagine a life where you're no longer held back by self-doubt or anxiety. You're no longer afraid to pursue your dreams, whether it's starting a business, building a meaningful relationship, or stepping into a leadership role. You're no longer waiting for the right moment to live fully and be fully yourself; you're creating it, every day.

THE COACHING CORNER

This is the "Living Fierce life"—a life that reflects the best version of you and allows you to step into the world with courage, authenticity, and purpose. My clients aren't just "surviving"; they're living. They embrace every challenge as an opportunity for growth and every moment as an opportunity to shine. By doing this they also get the joy of giving back and experiencing contribution to something greater than themselves. It's a total win/win.

The journey to living your Fierce Life doesn't end when our sessions do. It's a lifelong commitment to growth, self-love, and intentional living. And for my clients, it's the beginning of an unforgettable, empowered, and fulfilling life. As I always say: Refine- Every Day in Every Detail.

Time to Live Fierce!

This is your moment—don't let it pass. Can you see yourself energised, confident, and unstoppable, ready to take on anything or anyone that life throws your way?

If you're ready to leave self-doubt behind and step into the fierce new you, let's make it happen now!

Visit **www.IanNortonCoaching.com** to start your transformation. **Connect with me on Facebook, Instagram and LinkedIn for powerful insights and to join a community of others levelling up their lives. It's time—let's go!**

Website: www.IanNortonCoaching.com

Facebook: www.facebook.com/ijgnorton/

THE COACHING CORNER

Instagram: www.instagram.com/iannortonofficial/

LinkedIn: www.linkedin.com/in/ian-norton101/

Scan The QR Code

THE COACHING CORNER

Chapter 8

Beating the Odds: A Heartfelt Journey of Resilience, Purpose, and Authentic Leadership

By Ashley Harrison

My story

Born with a heart condition, I underwent groundbreaking open-heart surgery at just 10 days old—a procedure that had only been performed on four infants globally, with two survivors. My parents were faced with a very difficult decision: whether to go through with the surgery. However, the doctors made it clear that without it, I wouldn't survive. In many ways, the choice was made for them, and the surgery went ahead.

Thanks to the skill of an amazing cardiac team and extraordinary surgeon, I made it through and am here today to share my journey. I grew up with a spirit of resilience and determination, never letting

THE COACHING CORNER

anything hold me back. Raised in a large, busy, loving family, I found strength in that support, which helped me face every challenge that came my way.

I can only imagine what it was like for my parents and family with the amount of hospital visits and care I needed, but I recovered well and made a strong start in life. Always being sporty and healthy at school was important to me, and now I look back and realise it was the mind, body, heart connection which gave purpose to my life and the reason to keep a healthy body and healthy mind, little did I know, that this would help shape the person I am today.

My heart condition didn't go away, and I was closely monitored and looked after by two fantastic cardiac medical teams. It was always there, and something I had to be mindful of, however I often took on lots of things, with sport, life, family and was always on the go. The lead-up to my annual check-ups always brought a sense of anxiety and tension. My family and I couldn't help but wonder if this would be the visit where the doctors would tell us I needed further surgery. Hearing the words, "Ashley, you're good for now; we'll see you in another 12 months!" always brought immense relief and reassurance, allowing me to carry on with life as I knew it.

Leaving school, I went to university and subsequently into education as a teacher. I loved my job and quickly realised my calling was to make a difference to the children and communities I worked with. Whilst I loved my role as class teacher, I embraced many opportunities and embarked on my leadership journey. I knew I wanted to have a wider impact in education and for the future generations. I grew in my roles as a senior leader, a facilitator of a range of leadership and education programmes, an executive coach and I took schools on a journey of transformation and sustained improvement in my roles as Headteacher and Education Consultant.

I've always been passionate about learning myself and helping others to make a difference in their own lives and roles and that of others. As a result of this, not only did I embrace opportunities to progress in my career, but I also embraced opportunities for professional development which leads me to where I am today.

Completing a range of coaching qualifications, including those with Neuro-linguistic programming (NLP), Executive Coaching, Emotions Coaching, Systemic Team Coaching, Coaching with Embodiment and Physical Intelligence, and Coaching with Positive Intelligence.

Outside of my coaching professional development, I have completed my NPQEL (National Professional Qualification for Executive Leadership), Advanced Senior Mental Health for System Leadership, and I'm near completion of my Masters Degree in Leadership and Management, with the focus of my thesis based on the impact of coaching with Embodiment and Physical Intelligence. I really do love learning!

Change Makers for the Future

My parents and family have always been a great source of

THE COACHING CORNER

inspiration for me.

Family tea times were often filled with conversations about their work and business, which sparked my curiosity from an early age. Whilst my career initially began in education, I always knew that my larger vision was to build my own leadership coaching and consultancy business, empowering others to become the change-makers of the future.

I know only too well, that challenges are inevitable in life, but it's our responses that truly matter and can determine our growth and future path. My heart condition will always be part of my story, but it doesn't define who I am. The person I am today is defined by my values, the choices I make, the habits I develop, the relationships I nurture and the purpose that drives and inspires me. Who I am is shaped by my resilience in overcoming obstacles, my willingness to grow through life's experiences and my dedication to staying true to myself. Ultimately, it's the difference I make in the lives of others and the legacy I choose to create is what's important to me.

Throughout my life and career, I have always put my efforts and love into the needs of others and empowering them to grow and thrive, often before my own needs. However, in recent years, I recognised it was time to start prioritising my own well-being and self-care, just as I had advised others to do. Taking time for myself has strengthened my ability to support others, helped me stay grounded and has enabled me to be the best version of myself, showing up authentically in all aspects of my life. It has given me the opportunity to reflect and realign with my true purpose, which wasn't solely about being the leader in education anymore; this was about me as an individual. It was time to return to centre, back to my core, back to my soul.

In moments of deep reflection, I felt immense gratitude for the resilience and positivity my upbringing had instilled in me, and as I focused on self-care and the needs of my family, my vision for the future became clear. I felt deeply aligned with my purpose and ready to embark on the next stage of my journey of growth—not only for myself but for others too. It was time for me to create a legacy of change and it was from this place of clarity and purpose that BTD Coaching & Consultancy was born. Alongside it came BTD Leadership Academy for training and accreditation programs and BTD Leadership Hub, a community for practice, collaboration, and engagement.

This chapter of my life marked a turning point—one where I learned that real leadership begins with leading yourself first.

Why my coaching offer is so unique?

As a keen learner myself, and through my own personal experiences, I am always evolving and embedding high quality and creative ways to provide a service to empower others, accelerate growth and change in their personal or professional lives, whether this be on an individual level or an organisational level with a systemic view for improving work-based cultures, team development and stakeholder engagement to improve recruitment and retention.

THE COACHING CORNER

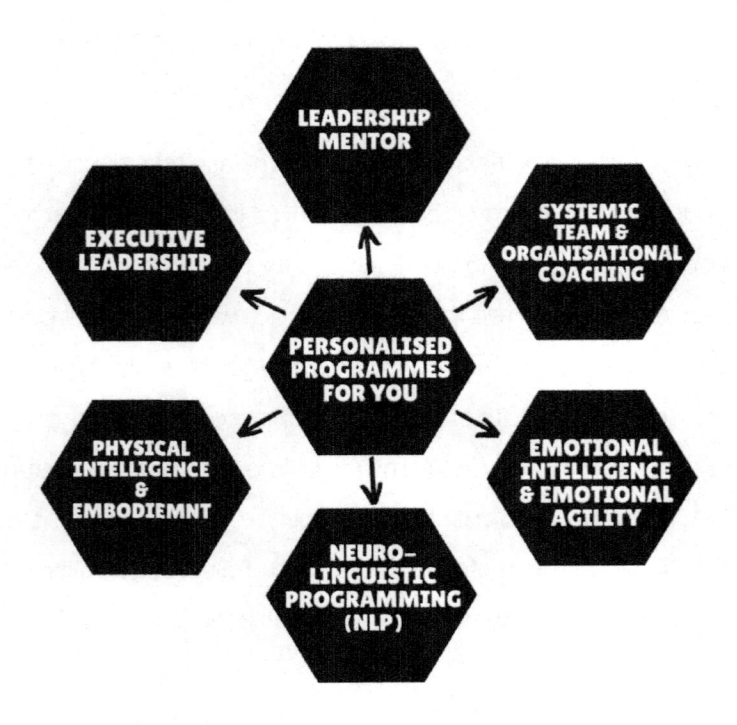

```
                LEADERSHIP
                 MENTOR

                              SYSTEMIC
   EXECUTIVE                  TEAM &
   LEADERSHIP                 ORGANISATIONAL
                              COACHING

                PERSONALISED
                PROGRAMMES
                  FOR YOU

   PHYSICAL                   EMOTIONAL
   INTELLIGENCE               INTELLIGENCE
   &                          & EMOTIONAL
   EMBODIEMNT                 AGILITY

                  NEURO-
                LINGUISTIC
                PROGRAMMING
                   (NLP)
```

As a qualified coach in the following areas of specialism, I create personalised coaching and leadership programmes with strategic development plans to enable clients to get the most out of their experience, by unlocking potential and nurturing growth of individuals, teams and organisations.

I will provide top tips to accelerate your leadership practice, help you gain confidence to secure your next leadership role and take you on a journey of transformation with insights of how I can help you become the best version of yourself and 🏃 **be the change you the wish to see in the world.**

THE COACHING CORNER

The Importance of Psychological Safety

When working with clients, I build a foundation of psychological safety with empathy and confidentiality, to create safe and supportive spaces for growth and to develop a deeper sense of self-awareness. I embrace curiosity and encourage clients to do the same, helping them to be comfortable in the unknown, and to explore what's underneath the surface.

As a coach and consultant, I work with leaders to develop their knowledge of psychological safety and their understanding that it isn't built over night, as it requires consistent effort, trust building and modelling from them as leaders.

The phrase 'Psychological Safety' first coined by Amy Edmundson refers to the team environment being safe for inter-personal risk taking and free to express ideas without fear of judgement.

Edmondson says. *"You no longer have the option of leading through fear or managing through fear. In an uncertain, interdependent world, it doesn't work—either as a motivator or as an enabler of high performance. It's literally mission critical in today's work environment."*

Why Psychological Safety Matters

1. **Enhances Innovation:** When team members feel safe, they're more likely to propose bold ideas and think creatively without fear of failure.
2. **Boosts Engagement:** Employees who feel

THE COACHING CORNER

psychologically safe are more engaged, as they trust their contributions are valued.

3. **Improves Decision-Making:** Teams with psychological safety can have candid discussions, leading to more robust decision-making and problem-solving.

4. **Encourages Learning from Mistakes:** A safe environment allows teams to reflect on errors and grow from them rather than hiding issues out of fear.

5. **Strengthens Collaboration:** Trust and openness create a foundation for deeper collaboration, where every voice is heard and valued.

Top Tips for Fostering Psychological Safety

1. Lead with Vulnerability

- Model the behaviour you want to see by admitting your own mistakes and sharing personal challenges.
- For example, say, "I got this wrong, but here's what I learned," to create a culture where it's safe to fail and grow.

2. Encourage Open Dialogue

- Actively solicit input from all team members, especially those who are quieter or hesitant to speak up.
- Use questions like, "What's your perspective on this?" or "What concerns might we not have considered?"

THE COACHING CORNER

3. Avoid Blame
   - Frame mistakes as opportunities for learning rather than assigning fault.
   - For example, instead of saying, "Who caused this problem?" ask, "What can we learn from this situation to prevent it in the future?"

4. Acknowledge and Value Contributions
   - Recognize and affirm contributions during discussions, even if you don't fully agree.
   - Use phrases like, "That's an interesting perspective," or "I appreciate you bringing that up—it's important to consider."

5. Set Clear Expectations for Respect
   - Establish team norms that prioritize respect and active listening. For instance, agree that interruptions are discouraged, and all ideas are treated with curiosity.
   - Facilitate team discussions to co-create these norms so everyone feels ownership.

6. Facilitate Inclusive Decision-Making
   - Use tools like brainstorming, anonymous feedback, or silent voting to ensure diverse input without fear of judgment.
   - For example, have everyone write down ideas on sticky notes before discussing them as a group.

7. Check in Regularly
   - Use regular one-on-ones or team check-ins to ask, "How safe do you feel sharing your ideas or concerns?"

THE COACHING CORNER

1. Address any hesitations directly and take action to improve the environment.

8. Practice Active Listening

- Listen fully to what others are saying without interrupting or
1. formulating your response prematurely.
2. Reflect back what you heard to ensure understanding: "What I hear you saying is..."

9. Celebrate Effort and Progress

- Recognize not just outcomes but the effort and courage it took for team members to speak up or take risks.
- For example, say, "I really appreciate how you raised that issue—it's not easy to do, but it's critical for our success."

Be The Change: As a leader, you have the power to unlock your team's full potential by fostering psychological safety—the foundation of innovation, engagement, and lasting success. This is your chance to create a work environment where individuals feel empowered to bring their whole selves, enhancing creativity, collaboration, and resilience. Build trust, openness, and the confidence needed to navigate challenges together, and watch your team thrive. Be the change maker of the future and lead the way in transforming workplace culture.

Coaching with Physical Intelligence (PI) & Embodiment: Unlocking the Body's Wisdom in Leadership

As a Physical Intelligence coach, I specialise in helping leaders, teams and organisations unlock their full potential by harnessing the powerful connection between the body and mind. Physical

THE COACHING CORNER

Intelligence (founded by Claire Dale) is about understanding how our body's biochemistry – hormones, neurotransmitters, and physical states – directly influences how we think, feel, and perform. When we learn to regulate these processes, we can significantly enhance our focus, resilience, emotional balance and overall effectiveness.

I highlight the value of embodied leadership and provide tools to manage stress, improve decision making and build resilience, exploring ways to lower stress hormones like cortisol, enabling clients to stay calm and composed in high pressure situations.

I encourage clients to reflect on how embodied leadership fosters trust, engagement and a deeper sense of presence and self-awareness, exploring ways to increase Oxytocin, Dopamine and DHEA empowering them to thrive in their own authentic style of leadership.

I help individuals and teams harness the innate intelligence of their bodies to optimise performance, focusing on building stronger collaboration, trust and alignment whilst embedding these practices into the wider culture.

Through tailored strategies, I help improve communication, emotional agility, and connection, creating environments where people feel energised, supported and motivated, leading to higher performance, sustainable well-being and greater value creation across organisations.

THE COACHING CORNER

Top Tips for becoming an embodied leader to create lasting change

1. **Body Scanning:** Explore body-scan meditations to notice areas of tension or ease. For example, "Close your eyes and scan from head to toe. What sensations do you notice in your shoulders or chest?" Regular practice increases self-awareness.

2. **Integrate Movement Practices:** Encourage activities like yoga, tai chi, or simply standing up and stretching during workdays. These practices reduce stress and help leaders reconnect to their physicality. Movement practices can have a positive impact and shift in state in little as 10 seconds, and regular 1 minute movement cycles can really transform your focus and energy.

3. **Focus on Posture:** Physical posture impacts perception. For example, a power pose (standing tall, open chest) can boost confidence before a presentation.

4. **Leverage Somatic Cues:** Recognise stress signals within your body like shallow breathing or fidgeting → practice intentional shifts, such as taking three deep belly breaths to reset.

5. **Practice Grounding:** "Four-Square Breathing" (inhale for four counts, hold for four, exhale for four, hold for four). This calms the nervous system, especially before high-pressure meetings.

THE COACHING CORNER

6. **Reflect on Energy:** Track how your energy shifts throughout the day. "Where do you feel it in your body?" Reflect on questions like, "When do you feel most alive and engaged?" and "What drains you?" to align work with energy patterns.

7. **Use Visualisation:** Explore visualisations of your ideal leadership presence. For example: "Imagine walking into a room as your most confident self. What do you notice about your posture, tone, and energy?"

8. **Reframe Feedback:** Remember to view feedback as data. Reflect with curiosity by asking, "What might this feedback teach you about how others perceive your leadership?"

🏃 **Be The Change:** This is your moment to lead with unshakable self-confidence grounded in physical awareness. Show others your ability to stay composed, respond effectively, and perform at your best in high-stakes situations. As an embodied leader, you'll experience holistic empowerment, alignment with your purpose, and an enhanced capacity to communicate and connect—both verbally and non-verbally. Unlock the power to release old patterns stored in the body and build sustainable habits for lasting success.

Cultivate improved focus, mental clarity, and physical resilience to thrive in demanding environments whilst preventing burnout. Step into your best self—start leading with purpose and presence today.

THE COACHING CORNER

Emotional Agility: Navigating the Human Side of Leadership

I help leaders master emotional intelligence and agility to strengthen relationships, enhance decision-making, promote self-regulation and improve leadership influence. By navigating the human side of leadership with empathy and awareness, leaders can better understand emotional dynamics, challenge perceptions, foster deeper connections and enhance creativity and innovation. This empowers them to foster trust, inclusivity, and shared purpose, creating thriving teams and organisations rooted in meaningful relationships.

Top tips for becoming an emotionally intelligent leader

- **Name Emotions:** Normalise emotions as part of leadership. For example, say, "Frustration is common in this situation. What might it be trying to tell you?" Naming emotions helps leaders gain perspective. Explore emotions using an emotions wheel or compass to navigate and gain a deeper sense of emotions which server you or hinder you.

- **Introduce Pause Practices:** Pause before reacting. For instance, count to five or take a sip of water during a heated moment. This simple pause can prevent reactive behaviour.

- **Roleplay Scenarios:** Use real-life examples to practice emotionally charged conversations. For example, rehearse how to deliver critical feedback with empathy and clarity.

THE COACHING CORNER

- **Cultivate Empathy:** Use exercises like imagining a situation from another person's perspective. Ask, "What might this person be feeling or needing right now?" to foster connection.

- **Set Boundaries:** Identify where you need to say "no" or

- delegate tasks to protect your energy and focus. Use phrases like, "What would saying 'yes' to this cost you?"

🏃 **Be The Change:** Step into the power of emotional agility and elevate your leadership. Gain heightened awareness of emotional triggers and patterns—both in yourself and others—and build resilience to navigate life's challenges and difficult emotions with confidence. This is your opportunity to lead with advanced interpersonal skills, establish healthy boundaries, and manage conflict effectively. With high emotional intelligence, you'll cultivate lasting emotional balance, maintain perspective, inspire disengaged teams, and adopt a solution-focused mindset to achieve your personal and professional goals. The future of impactful leadership starts with you.

Systemic Team Coaching (STC):

Building High-Value and High Performing Collaborative Cultures

As a Systemic Team Coach, I partner with teams and organisations to enhance collaboration, alignment, and collective performance by addressing team dynamics, relationships, stakeholder engagement, and broader systemic contexts. Each programme is

THE COACHING CORNER

tailored to the organisation's unique needs, offering strategic plans to navigate complexities, align goals and KPIs, and engage stakeholders effectively. Services may include team and leadership coaching, collaborative working initiatives, group coaching, and customised workshops designed to drive actionable outcomes and support the transformation journey.

🏃 **Be The Change:** Embrace the power of systemic team coaching to transform how you lead and collaborate. Align team dynamics with organisational goals to build resilience and navigate challenges effectively. Foster a culture of trust, shared accountability, and distributed leadership, empowering change and innovation across roles. Break down silos, enhance cross-functional collaboration, and drive sustainable team performance. Create a thriving culture of continuous learning that improves recruitment, retention, and long-term success. Take the next step in building high-value and high-performing teams to shape a better future for your organisation.

The Power of Purpose: Aligning Leadership with Vision and Values

No matter the path you take to accelerate your leadership journey, it always comes down to the power of purpose and alignment in both personal and professional life. For me, a life-changing experience brought me back to my centre, enabling me to be more present for my family, my purpose, and the leaders I'm called to work with.

THE COACHING CORNER

Do you wake up each day with clarity on your purpose, moral compass, and core values?

Do you embody and demonstrate these values to yourself, your family, and your community?

As this chapter closes, I encourage you to revisit your purpose, both as a person and as a leader. Purpose-driven values and leadership foster thriving cultures, driving engagement, innovation, and long-term success.

From a leadership perspective, here are some top tips for alignment

1. **Start with "Why":** Use Simon Sinek's Golden Circle model to explore the deeper "why" behind leadership goals. Ask, "What drives you to lead? What impact do you want to create? What legacy do you want to leave behind?"

2. **Align Decisions with Values:** Reflect on past decisions to identify core values. For instance, "What values were guiding you when you made that choice?" Consider using these values in future decision-making.

3. **Uncover Hidden Drivers:** Dig deeper by exploring personal stories. Reflect, "What experiences shaped your leadership philosophy?" Stories often reveal hidden motivations.

4. **Storytelling Exercises**: What's your story? What's happened in your life for you to end up in this role? What challenges and milestones have you experienced and overcome?

THE COACHING CORNER

Consider how you could articulate your purpose and vision in compelling ways.

5. **Reconnect to Purpose in Tough Times:** Consider reflective journaling or conversations to remember your "why" during setbacks. For example, "How does this challenge connect to your larger mission?"

🏃 **Be The Change:** When you realign with your vision and values, you tap into the transformative power of living and working with purpose. Everything—life and work—will gain clarity, bringing you balance and meaning in the present and as you look ahead.

This is your life, and you have the power to shape your own destiny. Seize the opportunity to be the change maker you're meant to be!

🏃 **Be the Change:** Are you ready to be the change makers of the future? If any of the 'Be the Change' sections resonated with you, then it's time to get in touch and start your journey of leadership transformation today!

Not quite ready...keep reading!

Transform How You Lead and Live

Did you know that leadership starts from within – when you grow, your team grows with you?

Did you know that how you feel directly impacts how you perform?

THE COACHING CORNER

Did you know that personal growth fuels team success and drives collective achievement?

By working with me you'll gain practical strategies to improve your leadership influence and unlock the connection between how you feel and how you lead. You'll learn how to elevate your performance, unleash your potential and lead with greater clarity, energy, purpose and confidence whilst creating balance and well-being for yourself and your organisation.

Your next leadership opportunity is closer than you think! Whether you are wanting to grow in your current role or keen to step into your next leadership position, our BTD Leadership Academy Programmes are designed to prepare you for success, equipping you with the skills, confidence and strategies to thrive and lead with impact.

Embark on your BTD journey with me today and become a self-aware leader who is a catalyst for positive change and leads with impact and authenticity.

Collaborate Better. Engage Stakeholders. Drive Growth

Systemic Team Coaching (STC) aligns organisations for long term success and helps them transform obstacles into opportunities. Together, we'll co-create solutions and strategies to improve cross-functional collaboration, overcome silos, engage stakeholders and create cultures of innovation whilst driving sustainable growth.

THE COACHING CORNER

Leadership isn't just about surviving or achieving – it's about thriving

Join the BTD Leadership Hub to gain access to expert advice, leadership resources, and a supportive network to help you grow, reflect and build your roadmap to success. Get ready to connect with a community of leaders dedicated to growth and impact!

Follow the link below for additional free content

'Be The Change: Golden Nuggets for Leadership Growth and Influence'

Linktree: https://linktr.ee/btdleadershipacademy

LinkedIn: Ashley Harrison

Instagram: @BTDLeadershipAcademy

Website: www.BTDCoachingandconsultancy.com

Website: www.BTDLeadershipAcademy.com

THE COACHING CORNER

Chapter 9

The Playful Coach Approach:

Using the Power of Playfulness to Navigate Complexity

By Sarah Creevey, The Playful Coach

Playing amongst the panic

In 2018 I had one of the most terrifying experiences of my life. I was on a plane coming into land when we hit extreme turbulence. My body left my seat several times as we were buffeted about. As I looked around I saw panic and fear across my fellow passengers' faces. People were screaming. Suddenly, the plane tipped sharply upwards, and the pilot's voice broke through on the tannoy. He told us he'd had to abort the landing. We were in the middle of a cyclone, he explained, and it was too dangerous to land. We'd have to stay in the air until the storm subsided. For what felt like an eternity, we continued to be flung back and forth, up and down

THE COACHING CORNER

inside that plane, the sounds of panic filling the cabin.

I knew I had a choice at that point: succumb to the fear, or do something to take myself away from it. I put my noise-cancelling headphones on, selected an upbeat 90s soundtrack that reminded me of fun times at uni, closed my eyes and imagined I was on a rollercoaster. From then on, every plunge was a thrilling drop, every stomach-lurching sway an exciting twist. In my mind, I was in a happy place, teetering on the exhilarating edge between fear and fun. And I kept my cool.

After the height of the storm had passed and the plane finally landed, I looked over at the passenger next to me. It was a woman. Calm, collected, though with a palpable look of relief in her eyes. I asked her how she had remained so composed throughout the terrifying experience we had just had. "I had to, really, for her," she said to me, signalling her young daughter on the seat next to her. Then I noticed what they were doing. Throughout the whole ordeal they had been playing word puzzles on their tablet. Mindfully distracted from the panic around them, compellingly occupied with creative problem solving instead. They, like me, had chosen to play amongst the panic.

This experience stayed with me not just because of its intensity, but because it revealed something universal: even in moments of great uncertainty, we have the power to choose how we respond. What if you could apply that same principle to your own challenges? Whether it's navigating career pressures, finding clarity in a complex decision, or managing the stresses of leadership, the ability to shift perspective—like reframing turbulence as a rollercoaster—can be transformational. This is where playfulness comes in.

In the pages ahead, I'll show you how The Playful Coach Approach can lead to powerful breakthroughs—empowering you to navigate the complexities of life and work with confidence and creativity.

Discovering my playful calling

At this point, I should probably explain a little more about why I became a coach. Unlike many executive coaches, I do not have a background in HR. The first part of my career was spent in market research agencies. My job was to help businesses understand their customers better and to develop products, services and strategies based on this insight. The work was varied and interesting. I was good at my job, always receiving good feedback from clients and getting several promotions. But, as anyone who has worked in client services knows, agency life can be a lot of fun, *and* highly stressful. After 10 years working in this pressurised environment, now leading my own team, I experienced burnout. I found myself losing all motivation for the work I had previously enjoyed and felt unable to cope with the plate-spinning act I had perfected over the last few years. The crunch point came when I started to take time off for psycho-somatic symptoms linked to stress. I knew something had to change. I learned about positive psychology and how to intentionally improve my own well-being. At work, I listened to the familiar complaints about stress and overwhelm from my team and I realised that I wanted to help prevent others getting to the same

THE COACHING CORNER

point of collapse I had got to. I wanted to help people enjoy their jobs. And so I retrained as a coach.

At around the same time, I signed up for a course in theatre improvisation (improv) near to my work. I had a degree in drama and had always been curious to give improv a go so this seemed like an opportune time. I somehow knew it would be a useful skill to learn as a coach, but I hadn't banked on it improving my well-being so much.

Each class was like therapy for me. As I continued to sign up for more courses, eventually progressing to public performances, I became more and more curious about why it had such a profound impact. Was it the meeting of other like-minded people? To an extent. Was it an escape from my daily stressors? Partly. But above all, I realised there was something else – it gave me *permission to play*.

The art of Improv Is about fully entering the moment, being open to whatever happens, letting go of trying to get it "right" and enjoying the process without focusing on the outcome. This is the same state of mind children take on during explorative play. More than just providing me with a useful set of skills for my coaching and facilitation practices, learning improv taught me the importance of being allowed to play as an adult, and that has informed my approach to my work – and my research – ever since.

THE COACHING CORNER

A moment to reflect...

Before we go any further, I'd like to offer you a moment to reflect. Where in your life as an adult do you make space for play?

I don't mean being part of a sports team on a Tuesday night (that has many great benefits but for a different reason). I mean playing in the way you used to as a child, without imposed rules and structure, with permission to be and do whatever you feel in the moment, with no particular outcome in mind. Maybe that means you're splashing in puddles, or skimming stones, or dancing around your living room like no one is watching. It's doing whatever you do with gay abandon.

In my experience, we tend to do less of this stuff as we get older, and even less so deliberately dedicate time to it. Life gets in the way. And when life means the serious business of going to work, impressing clients and leading teams, "being playful" just doesn't feature.

But imagine now how your life would be if you did dedicate time to pure play, the kind where you just let yourself go without needing to worry about the outcome. Perhaps that brings a smile to your face. Perhaps you notice a tightening up in your muscles at the idea. Perhaps you think I'm off my rocker and want to move on to the next chapter right now!

Whatever your response, notice it and be curious. If it's caused a reaction in you in any way, you're already experiencing some of the power of playfulness. I urge you to hold that lightly and read on while I add a bit more seriousness to all this talk about play.

THE COACHING CORNER

Here's The Science Bit

We are hard wired to play. Some scientists believe that our playfulness is what sets us apart as a species, not because we are the only species to play (we are not) but because we play for longer in our life cycle than any other animal. It is through play in childhood that we learn to adapt to our environment. We develop resilience, empathy, cognition and emotional awareness. We learn how to relate to others, ourselves and the world around us. Children play in every culture across the world. Playing is our in-built mechanism for learning and growth.

All this makes sense, but what about once we're adults? Sure, it can be fun to still play sometimes, but surely it stops being so important. You might think so. But insofar as we still need to learn and grow in adulthood, it still helps us to be playful. In fact, several research studies have found clear benefits to being a playful adult. Below are a few examples:

- A 2016 study examined the Red Hat Society, a community for women over 50 known for its playful culture. The study found that as members' playfulness increased over time, so did their resilience, concluding that playfulness can help to build resilience even in adulthood.[1]
- A 2021 experiment asked adults to complete playful tasks over a week. The results showed improved well-being and reduced depressive symptoms. The researchers concluded that adopting playfulness as adults in everyday life could help prevent depression and boost happiness.[2]

THE COACHING CORNER

- In 2007, a study with professionals across a range of sectors including media, education, tech, agriculture and manufacturing found that playful workers were more innovative, performed better in their jobs and were happier at work. The researchers recommended that workplaces create more playful environments to improve the motivation and the performance of their employees.[3]
- Two studies, one from 1994 and one from 2018, found that playful language used in task instructions affected people's experience of completing the task and the quality of their outputs. This suggests that when we have a more playful mindset we are more motivated, more likely to enjoy the activity we are doing and likely to think more creatively.[4,5]

All this tells me that playfulness is something we need to take seriously, no matter our age. It also indicates that it's just as relevant at work as elsewhere. It says we can improve our enjoyment of, motivation for and performance at work just by shifting our mindset to "play". There's even a name for doing that, coined by a group of Organisational Psychologists from The Netherlands: Playful Work Design.[6]

As an executive coach working with people in their professional environments, I see a discernible shift when I give my clients permission to be playful. Being playful means bringing an attitude of playfulness to whatever topic we are discussing – an openness, a spontaneity, a freeing up of constraints. It taps into that innate drive for play we all share.

THE COACHING CORNER

But there's more to playfulness than just a shift in mindset. When we adopt a playful attitude, we enter what psychologists call a "play state." In this state, we feel safe to experiment, explore new ideas, and take risks without fear of failure. This is what children do when they pretend to be superheroes or doctors—they're rehearsing life skills in a low-stakes environment. What's more, psychologists believe that the more often we enter these play states, the more playful we become,[7] and so we create a virtuous upward spiral. That's what was happening to me in my improv class – I was exercising my playfulness "muscle", which helped me to bring a more playful attitude to other areas of my life, freed up my thinking and improved my overall well-being and resilience.

Cut to the plane, and, although I didn't realise it at the time, my instinct to ride an imaginary rollercoaster instead of succumb to panic came from having a well-exercised playfulness muscle.

Imagine applying all this to your own life. What if you could "try on" leadership strategies or practice tough decisions in a playful way before committing to them? How might that improve your confidence and clarity? Or what if you could inject positive energy into difficult tasks by viewing them as play? How might that reduce the stress they cause you?

In my experience, most adults don't give themselves permission to experiment this way, yet doing so can be incredibly empowering. That's where The Playful Coach Approach comes in.

THE COACHING CORNER

The Playful Coach Approach

Executive coaching of any kind can be described as an intrinsically playful process. It relies on the coach being present, open and curious about what might come up, and results in creative thinking from the client. It takes a certain degree of playfulness, from both the coach and the client, to create a space where all these things can happen. Moreover, since playfulness is our natural mechanism for learning and growth, and coaching is a real-time process of learning, it makes complete sense that coaching should help clients tap into their own playfulness in order to learn.

The world of therapy appears to have known this for some time. In developing The Playful Coach Approach, I looked to the work of Donald Winnicott,[8] a psychoanalyst well known for emphasising the importance of play. While Winnicott's ideas originated in therapy, they provide a useful framework for understanding how playfulness creates a safe space for exploration and growth that is also relevant for coaching (italics indicate where I have changed Winnicott's words to my own):

> *Coaching* takes place in the overlap of two areas of playing, that of the *coachee* and that of the *coach*. *Coaching* has to do with two people playing together. The corollary of this is that where playing is not the *norm* then the work done by the *coach* is directed towards *creating a space where both coach and coachee have permission to play together with a shared goal of exploration and learning.*

THE COACHING CORNER

When I work with clients using The Playful Coach Approach, I invite them to play. From this playful place — this "play state" - they are able to explore new thoughts, ideas and actions with complete freedom. So, although the coaching may physically take place in a meeting room or on a Zoom call, it should feel more like entering a playground than a business meeting. This is where I see transformation happen.

Playfulness, then, is not about playing games but about entering a mindset or attitude in which possibilities become endless and can be explored with freedom. There are 5 components to playfulness: creativity, spontaneity, pleasure, curiosity and humour,[9] and any or all of these can be brought into a coaching session to make it playful. The Playful Coach Approach suggests this can be done in one of three ways, by *thinking, doing* or *being.*

Thinking

This is about inviting the client to think playfully about their current challenge. In coaching jargon, we call this using a playful "lens." I might subtly change my language to encourage a more playful mindset (e.g. "What would you like to play with today?"), or I might ask a more overt question to get them to think about the challenge as something playful. You can try this out for yourself with the following example:

- Think of a challenge you are currently feeling stuck with and write it down.

THE COACHING CORNER

- What are the most important parts of the challenge to play with (explore)? Which do you want to play with (explore) most?
- If this challenge was a game, what would be the rules? Who would the players be? How could you win?
- If you just wanted to enjoy this challenge, regardless of winning, how could you approach it?

Doing

This is about actively doing something playful while exploring the challenge at hand. This may be having a conventional coaching conversation while doing something physical, such as playing catch, walking in nature or even swinging on swings (I've never yet coached a client in a real playground but would love to try this!) Alternatively, the playful activity could be *about* the challenge, so you might draw, write or build something that represents the challenge in some way. Why not give this a go too?

- Thinking of the same challenge as above, or taking a new one, how could you draw this? (alternatively, see what it's like to build it with Playdoh or Lego)[10]
- What's missing from your creation?
- If it was in an art gallery, what would the title and caption be?
- What needs to change about your creation for your challenge to feel easier?

If that feels like too big a creative stretch for you, try just having a

THE COACHING CORNER

conversation about the challenge with a friend you trust while doing something fun and notice if anything unexpected comes up (if it does, please get in touch and share your experience, I'd love to hear about it!)

Being

This is the subtlest part of the approach because it's about something that is created between the coach and the client that cannot easily be captured. You know that playful energy you feel when you are having a good time with someone you trust? It's a way of being together and pervades all interactions. It might manifest in friendly humour or mischievous challenge from the coach but is always built on a firm basis of trust and respect. It's the part that signals the permission is there to really play together, and allows the Thinking and Doing parts described above to be fully entered into by both the coach and the client.

This is hard to try for yourself because it relies on having a partner. Have a think about who you can rely on for some playful energy and see what it's like to chat through a serious challenge with them. What new perspectives has their playfulness brought to light?

Playfulness in practice

I hope this chapter has intrigued you enough to consider using playfulness as a way to explore your challenges. In case you need more convincing, or are just interested to hear more, I'd like to finish

THE COACHING CORNER

by sharing 3 examples that stick in my mind of when The Playful Coach Approach has really shifted perspectives for clients of mine.

1. Taming the Fear Dragon

I'd been working some time with one client when he said he had a presentation coming up and was "going to die" when he gave it. "Really?" I said. I drew a stick character being killed and told him that was him dying giving his presentation. Immediately, he laughed because it was a) ridiculous and b) not a very good drawing. By playing with the idea of dying giving a presentation, he was able to release some of the fear around it and see it as something more manageable. Plus, he now had a comedic image he could recall when he felt the fear rising in him again.

2. "After the session I had an epiphany...."

After a workshop I ran on playfulness I received some feedback from a delegate that gave me goosebumps. She had been quite cautious in the workshop so I wasn't sure how she had found it. Her feedback told me that by reconnecting with a playfulness she had forgotten about she'd let go of some fairly big stuff from her past that had been holding her back. She described how much her mindset had changed and she was able to enjoy the present and use her own playfulness to bring joy into both her work and her personal life.

3. The Stardust CEO

A CEO I was working with described some quite complex issues he

THE COACHING CORNER

was having in the company he had grown over the last 25 years. I got him to stand up and indicate where he was in relation to the other parts of the business using the space around him, and then to enact his role in relation to all those business units. He started to spin around miming sprinkling stardust over each of them. We didn't talk much about the complexities of the various dynamics, we didn't need to. He was just in the middle of the room, sprinkling imaginary stardust and, suddenly, he knew what he needed to do in a way he hadn't been able to grasp before. He had played with it and the answer had come!

Are you ready to play?

I hope you have enjoyed this chapter and reading about how coaching with playfulness has the power to transform the way you approach life's challenges. I work (or rather play!) with both individuals and groups, particularly leaders and new managers who are navigating complexity. Whether you are experiencing the turbulence of a major change or simply seeking a fresh perspective, I'd love to help you discover the power of playful exploration. I invite you to visit my website or LinkedIn and get in touch if you'd like to know more. I'd love to hear from you!

www.theplayfulcoach.com

www.linkedin.com/in/sarahcreevey

THE COACHING CORNER

[1] Chang, P. J., Yarnal, C., & Chick, G. (2016). The longitudinal association between playfulness and resilience in older women engaged in the red hat society. *Journal of Leisure Research*, 48(3), 210-227

[2] Proyer, R. T., Gander, F., Brauer, K., & Chick, G. (2021). Can Playfulness be Stimulated? A Randomised Placebo-Controlled Online Playfulness Intervention Study on Effects on Trait Playfulness, Well-Being, and Depression. *Applied Psychology : Health and Well-Being*, 13(1), 129–151.

[3] Yu, P., Wu, J-J., Chen, I-H. and Lin, Y-T. (2007) Is playfulness a benefit to work? Empirical evidence of professionals in Taiwan. *International Journal of Technology Management*, 39(3/4), 412-429.

[4] Glynn, M. A. (1994). Effects of work task cues and play task cues on information processing, judgment, and motivation. *Journal of Applied Psychology*, 79(1), 34.

[5] Heimann, K.S., & Roepstorff, A. (2018). How Playfulness Motivates – Putative Looping Effects of Autonomy and Surprise Revealed by Micro Phenomenological Investigations. *Frontiers in Psychology*, 9, 1704.

[6] Bakker, A. B., Scharp, Y. S., Breevaart, K., & De Vries, J. D. (2020). Playful work design: Introduction of a new concept. *The Spanish Journal of Psychology*, 23, e19.

[7] Shen, X. (2020). Constructing an interactionist framework for playfulness research: Adding psychological situations and playful states. *Journal of Leisure Research*, 51(5), 536-558.

[8] Winnicott, D. W. (1971). *Playing and reality*. Basic Books.

[9] Guitard, P., Ferland, F., & Dutil, É. (2005). Toward a better understanding of playfulness in adults. OTJR: *Occupation, Participation and Health*, 25(1), 9-22.

[10] Play-Doh® is a trademark of Hasbro,Inc., and LEGO® is a trademark of LEGO Group, both used here for illustrative purposes.

THE COACHING CORNER

THE COACHING CORNER

Chapter 10

Grow as you go: How to create a career that works for you

By Katy Walton

Learning & Development Specialist and Leadership Coach. Founder and Director of Make Real Progress Ltd.

The adventure begins

Little did I know, as I set off with my rucksack on my back en route to Paris, that the summer ahead would change my life and my career.

I'm fascinated by how different career opportunities open up to us through our experiences, connections and learning. In this chapter, I'm sharing some of mine, along with a model I've created to help you navigate your own career choices.

My story starts whilst travelling in Australia.

THE COACHING CORNER

With a return flight date to the UK looming, I realised I wasn't quite ready to come back. I'd been over there for 11 months and felt like I had everything to stay for and no reason to leave. So, despite having very little funds, I took a punt that I'd be able to scrape enough together for a new ticket and decided to stay another 4 weeks, the limit of my visa.

Originally, I'd been due to fly into London and the cheapest new alternative took me to Manchester. And that twist changed everything.

I'd caught the travelling bug at a young age. My Dad had been in the Merchant Navy, away for months at a time. I'd get postcards from all over the World, hear stories of his adventures, and I knew instinctively that this was what I wanted to do when I grew up and I was impatient to get started.

Couple this with my Mum's experience (she had me at 18 and with the responsibility, felt like she'd lost her opportunity to travel) and you've got two parents who fully supported my decision to go out after college and explore instead of heading to university.

Over the next few years, I had a blast. Yes, I got to see some incredible sights (hello Barrier Reef, Sahara Desert and Bangkok street markets). Yes, I had some hairy experiences (hello midnight flood rescues in the South of France, terrorist activity and border police interrogations in Israel and Egypt). But importantly, I learnt from it.

- I learnt that I was capable, resourceful and self-sufficient

- I learnt the ability to connect with people of all nationalities, faiths, orientations and backgrounds
- I learnt how to have difficult and open conversations
- I learnt how to lead teams through both good and challenging times

All of which set the foundations for my opportunistic career [taking opportunities as they came, rather than planning career steps].

Landing back in Manchester, my good friend Gary came to greet me at the airport. We'd met a few years before when he joined the team of holiday reps I led on a campsite near Bordeaux and stayed in touch – no mean feat in the days before the internet.

Whilst staying with him, I headed out for lunch with other ex-colleagues and was offered a role in the Manchester based office of the travel company I'd worked for previously, which would then relocate to Paris in 3 months.

The role? Designing (in Manchester) and delivering (in Paris) training for campsite supervisors and holiday reps. The start of a career that I've truly loved, which stemmed from a love for travel, great connections and developing skills on the way.

A Parisian high

It's hard to capture in such a small space of time just how much I learnt from that summer in Paris. As a team of ten, we were trusted and empowered by our manager in Manchester to support and guide 100 young people every three days, at the start of their

THE COACHING CORNER

summer season as a holiday rep – many of whom were away from their homes for the first time.

With the responsibility to develop their skillsets in everything from paediatric first aid to wiring plugs. From leading teams to handling customer complaints. And that's before we even get started on the pastoral care.

I'd spend evenings with the trainees, building up the confidence of those grappling with anxiety, talking down people from situations escalated by alcohol, helping them to unravel their worries, and tensions, and listening to their excited plans.

We learnt to live, work and collaborate 24/7, all pulling together to achieve a common goal. The true definition of a high performing team.

Over the course of that summer, we jointly trained around 1800 folk at the Paris centre and each trainer had an area to support for ongoing coaching and guidance. What I'd learnt from travelling was immensely valuable and I built on that through every single experience and unexpected crisis that was thrown my way.

Like dealing with over a hundred reps stranded across France when a flash train strike occurred on travel day, before the days of mobile phones!

- I learnt how to create and facilitate a broad range of workshops

- I learnt how to apply my resourcefulness to unexpected challenges
- I learnt how to inspire confidence, motivate and the power of empathy
- I learnt the positive impact of psychological safety and empowerment as a team member

Paris was a true high point in my life. Not only for kick-starting my career in L&D (Learning and Development), as it was here that I met my husband, Paul.

But just two summers later, my World as I knew it would shatter.

The day I realised that Family comes first

I'd never felt as shocked or as lost.

My Dad who'd inspired my travels, the strong guy who knew how to fix pretty much anything, the man who - despite not being my biological Father – had taken me on and loved me like I was his own, was shrinking before our eyes.

He was in immense pain and told consistently he just had a bad back. When we finally convinced the Doctors to run more in-depth tests, they discovered Pancreatic Cancer.

And six days later, he passed away aged 48.

The day he died, Paul and I were travelling home on a Sunday evening after spending the weekend with him in hospital in Norfolk. I was one week into a new L&D role based in Peterborough and

THE COACHING CORNER

although I hadn't wanted to leave, I believed that we still had years with him and that he'd be going through treatment after his discharge the next day.

Just one hour after we left, we got a call telling us he'd taken a turn for the worse and we needed to get back there immediately. By the time we got back to him, he was unconscious until he slipped away a short while after.

The shock hit immediately. I didn't know what to think, do or say. But overriding all of that was the sudden realisation that I'd never be able to speak to him again. There were so many things I wish I'd told him and would never have the chance to.

It was a monumental time for me. Yet for everyone (family aside) around me, life continued pretty much as normal. For the first time in my life, I was acutely aware of the fragility of life and how deeply I loved my family.

I realised that many people didn't know what to say, to the extent that they'd avoid speaking to me. If you've ever experienced your own grief, you may recognise that too.

The greatest gift I believe you can ever give to someone in loss is to be there alongside them and listen. You don't need to say anything at all. I'm forever grateful that Paul did exactly this for me.

The trouble is, that many people want to help by 'fixing' things. Sharing platitudes, trying to snap you out of sadness.

THE COACHING CORNER

'Being present' and giving people space to vent, share, and talk is not as easy as it might sound. It's a core, critical skill and one of the most valuable skills to hone for your life and your career.

It can make the difference between colleagues feeling seen, heard and understood and wanting to walk out.

It can save friendships, workplace relationships, marriages and lives. And it's all too often overlooked, underappreciated and underutilised.

> *"Most people do not listen with the intent to understand; they listen with the intent to reply"* – Stephen Covey.

Whatever we experience, we can always choose to learn from it. Using those insights to shape our actions and decisions moving forward.

- I learnt that life is fragile and to not take anything or anyone for granted.
- I learnt to prioritise family above career.
- I learnt to have conversations that matter before it's too late.
- I learnt the real value of genuinely listening to others.

You can't read the label from inside the jar

With six years L&D experience under my belt, I joined a large financial services provider to bring management development expertise into the training team.

I was facilitating leadership and team development programmes

THE COACHING CORNER

full-time, learning from colleagues, external providers we partnered with, and from every single programme I led.

I was in 'in the flow' and I loved it.

As my skillset grew, I gained more opportunities and won in-house awards. Yet, ironically, the more recognition I gained the more of an imposter I felt.

Why was it that others believed I had strengths that I just couldn't see myself? I convinced myself that any minute I'd be exposed as a fraud. Everyone would realise they'd overestimated my ability.

I started to compare myself to others, seeing their outward confidence and capabilities, totally under-appreciating my own.

I started to convince myself I didn't belong there.

For a few years, I talked to myself in a way I'd never talk to others. Harsh words of criticism. Demanding perfection. Highlighting all the gaps.

My self-worth and confidence were on the floor.

I knew something needed to change, but I didn't know how. So, I found a mentor. I needed someone with experience, I wanted someone who would challenge me and help me turn it around.

And that person was Amanda. To this day, I'm not sure she fully recognises what a profound impact she had on my life (and yes, I have told her).

- She encouraged me to see different perspectives

- She encouraged me to focus on developing my strengths
- She encouraged me to focus on what would bring me happiness

I realised that sometimes you need someone else to help you see the things you can't see for yourself.

As a direct result of those conversations, I chose to take a PGCert in Coaching – formalising the on-the-job coaching experience I'd built in my L&D role.

To say it was transformative is an understatement.

As we dug deep into the Neuroscience and explored the wide range of Coaching and Therapeutic models, I began to learn much more about myself. Where and how my mindset was holding me back. What I'd chosen to believe and how I could choose to think differently.

Of course, the key to any learning is in the practical application, so working with volunteer coaching clients was a core element of the programme. Luckily, in a company with 20,000 employees, there was no shortage of people leaders to work with.

Which then led to perhaps the biggest learning of all.

People I'd placed on a pedestal (the most senior leaders) were almost always trying to find their own way themselves, even if appearing outwardly confident. Nobody had all the answers. Nobody felt like they got it right all the time.

It wasn't just me.

THE COACHING CORNER

I realised the power of vulnerability and openness. How sharing what we perceive as our weaknesses can, in fact, strengthen us and our working relationships.

It was a huge privilege to coach these leaders and see their transformations. At the same time, by sharing their experiences, they were transforming me. For the first time in years, through the combination of normalising the feelings of self-doubt and understanding its origin, it started to fade.

- I learnt that nobody is immune to self-doubt, especially in times of challenge and change.
- I learnt the real power of mentoring and coaching.
- I learnt that our mindset shapes how we see the World, what we do and who we become.
- I learnt the impact of dropping the professional mask and connecting person to person.

The big leap

'Life expands or shrinks according to one's courage' – **Anais Nin**

During the first Covid lockdown in 2020, like many others, I started to think about what I wanted from my life post-pandemic. By this point, I'd been working in Corporate L&D roles for 25 years across a range of companies.

I was 48. The age my dad had been when he died, which hit me like a ton of bricks. Life is too short, and I wasn't happy.

I'd recently accepted a promotion to lead an L&D team. The role

THE COACHING CORNER

demanded a focus on strategy, reports, budgets and planning, with significantly less time doing the work I loved and had great success with. Developing people.

With a shock, I realised I'd sleep-walked into a role that didn't bring me joy or play to my strengths. Life had become, as the French describe: "Metro, Boulot, Dodo" (commute, work, sleep).

For the first time, I'd made a career move because it was expected of me, without considering the implications. I didn't consider:

1. What do I **NEED** from my career to feel satisfied?
2. What gives me **ENERGY** and joy in my work?
3. What are my **STRENGTHS**?
4. What are my **WATCHOUTS**? (blind spots, or potential de-railers)

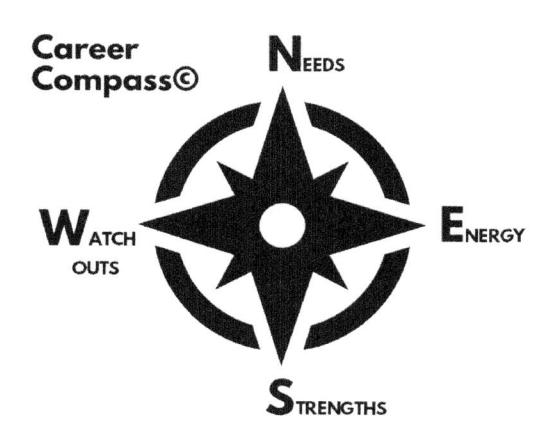

Career Compass©

- **N**EEDS
- **E**NERGY
- **S**TRENGTHS
- **W**ATCH OUTS

THE COACHING CORNER

I'd created the Career Compass to help people managers to have Cracking Career Conversations® with their teams and it was high time I reflected on it for myself.

Having already toyed with the idea of running my own business, I wondered if it would be a good fit for me at this stage in my life and career.

This is what I uncovered:

1. What are my career **Needs** right now? Autonomy, Balance, Creativity, Flexibility, and Friendships.
2. What gives me **Energy**? Facilitating, Training, and Coaching.
3. What are my **Strengths**? All the above plus building partnerships and relationships.
4. What are my **Watchouts**? Lack of business experience, practical financial knowledge, and navigating the challenges without colleagues.

Running a development and coaching business felt like a clear fit for Needs, Strength and Energy, but I knew I'd need to find a way to manage or develop the areas that were Watchouts, plus ensure that I still had friendships and support even when working by myself.

When I looked back at my career, I realised I'd already navigated challenges numerous times. If I'd done it before, I could do it again.

So, I got stuck straight in, learning all I could about setting up a business whilst at the same time, building up my network and making new connections.

I joined communities, even starting one of my own. I met phenomenal people doing amazing work. With each new connection, I learnt something new or generated more opportunities.

In the past few years since setting up my business, **Make Real Progress,** the learning curve has been steep to say the least. But it's without doubt one of the best career choices I've made.

- I learnt that courage is not the absence of fear, but acting in spite of it.
- I learnt the power of collaboration.
- I learnt how to start, build and grow a successful business.
- I learnt that everything I'd experienced in my career had led to this next chapter.

Making conscious choices

We're growing as we go.

Whatever path we choose to take after school and whatever decisions we make throughout our careers; every experience we have and every person we learn from shapes us for the future.

They help us to understand what we want and don't want from our current role and our next step.

THE COACHING CORNER

They help open the doors for opportunities that we can't yet see.

They help us to become more conscious in our choices.

'Until you make the unconscious conscious, it will direct your life, and you will call it fate' – Carl Jung.

For example, after the experience I'd had the day my dad died, I knew that family was my top priority. So, for years (until that final role) my career choices had revolved around my 'Need' for balance and to be there for my children. Which made it easier for me to decide to stay in roles at the same level that I was well-suited to. They played to Strengths, gave me Energy and my key Need was satisfied, so I could turn down job offers and promotions, without regrets.

Sure, other roles would have meant a bigger salary and more status. But I knew with certainty that Balance was my key priority. Anything else was a 'nice to have'.

When my eldest son didn't know his next step after school, we focussed on his Needs, Strengths and what gave him Energy. It didn't have to lead to a 'forever' career, but it did give him the space to experience more of the World before he chose a path that felt right for him.

Maybe now more than ever (with the uncertainty in this world, pace of change, and advances in technology) it's more helpful to focus on creating an opportunistic career, rather than planning longer term for a specific role that may not even exist in its current format

THE COACHING CORNER

in five years' time. It also helps to reduce the frustration of not seeing the next perfect role for you in an organisation.

By developing transferable skills (like coaching, resilience or communication) keeping yourself future fit, building great networks and connections – you're getting yourself ready for the next career opportunity when it presents itself. One that's right for you.

When I look back on my own career, I can clearly see what I learnt from each experience and how they've collectively shaped the path for what I offer through my business now:

1. **Supporting managers to lead, develop and inspire their teams**

By developing managers to strengthen their leadership capabilities and confidence, not only does it make a fundamental difference to them personally, but also the teams they lead and the organisations they work for (hello increased engagement, performance and retention!). And through 30 years of leading others, being led and working with leaders, I've seen the patterns that lead to success or failure.

2. **Supporting Coaches and HR professionals to build workshops and training programmes that get results for Corporate Clients.**

I support Coaches and HR professionals through sharing the practical tools and know-how from my experience in L&D, so they're easily able to create and run workshops. I never want a lack

THE COACHING CORNER

of confidence or experience hold them back from getting their valuable insights into the World!

So, here's to you and your career, whatever it is that you do.

You'll know from this chapter that I'm all for building relationships, so I'd love to invite you to connect with me.

And if you'd like my support so that you, or the leaders you work with can Make Real Progress, I'd be delighted to help.

Website: https://makerealprogress.co.uk/

LinkedIn: https://www.linkedin.com/in/katy-walton-make-real-progress/

LinkedIn

LinkedIn

Website

THE COACHING CORNER

Chapter 11

Rewrite Your Story, Redefine Your Life

By Jennifer Anderson

Finding My Calling

For so many women, life feels like an endless loop of obligations. You say yes when you want to say no. You put everyone else's needs before your own and wonder why you feel so drained. Deep down, you want more—but the idea of putting yourself first feels selfish, or worse, impossible.

Have you ever felt like you're living for everyone else but yourself? What would your life look like if you started putting yourself first?

I understand because I've been there. For years, I doubted myself, believed I wasn't good enough, and let others' expectations shape my life. But what if I told you it doesn't have to be this way? What

THE COACHING CORNER

if you could create a life where you're both respected and joyful, a life where you're free to pursue your dreams guilt-free? This is what I help women like you achieve.

Once I began to see my worth, I discovered that helping others find their footing gave me an unmatched sense of purpose. It wasn't just about setting goals or saying no to things that drained me—it was about believing I was worthy of setting boundaries and pursuing my bliss. That shift in belief became the foundation of my life and my coaching.

For years, I had been the go-to person for friends, coworkers, and even strangers who needed someone to listen. I thought this role was just something I was destined for, not something that could become my calling. What I didn't realize at the time was that I was honing a skill: the art of presence.

It wasn't until someone close to me pointed out how naturally trusted I was that I began to see my own value. Even strangers could sense that I was a safe place for their burdens. They didn't need me to fix anything—they just needed to feel heard.

That realization was eye-opening, but it wasn't the whole story. I still had to overcome the nagging voice in my head that told me I wasn't good enough to turn this gift into something meaningful. It wasn't until I started questioning that voice—challenging its assumptions—that I began to rewrite my narrative.

THE COACHING CORNER

If you're reading this and thinking, 'That sounds great, but I'm not sure I can do it,' I want you to know that I've been there. Every client I've worked with has felt the same way at the start. Change can feel overwhelming, but it starts with one small step. And you don't have to do it alone, that's why I'm here.

Journal Prompt:

- *Think about a time when you felt deeply valued by someone else. What did they see in you that you may not yet see in yourself?*

Finding My Way

The first thing I realized pretty quickly was that I still had work to do on myself. I had spent over thirty years living a story of mediocrity, and it was time to rewrite that script.

One story, in particular, had held me back for decades: the belief that I wasn't smart enough. It started in childhood when a friend constantly compared our intelligence and belittled me. Her voice stayed in my head, popping up whenever I faced a challenge, until I stopped trying altogether.

This belief didn't just affect my career aspirations—it seeped into every corner of my life. I doubted my ability to make good decisions, avoided taking risks, and constantly second-guessed myself. The moment I acknowledged how much this story was holding me back was the moment everything began to change.

THE COACHING CORNER

When I first started questioning my limiting beliefs, it was terrifying. The voice in my head would scream, 'What if you fail?' or "What if you let everyone down?' But I realized that staying stuck in those beliefs was even scarier. Change didn't happen overnight, but with every small step, I felt a little stronger and a little more like the person I was meant to be.

This is how I started building my first course, Overcoming Self-Doubt, I didn't just teach others to challenge their beliefs, I practiced what I preached. Slowly but surely, I started collecting evidence that proved my story wrong. Every time I succeeded at something I thought I couldn't do; I added it to my mental "proof list." Over time, those small wins grew into undeniable proof that I was smart, capable, and worthy of joy and success.

Why My Approach is Unique

My journey taught me that transformation is possible for anyone—but it takes the right guidance and tools. What sets my coaching apart is that I've been where you are. I know what it's like to feel stuck, to doubt your worth, and to wonder if change is possible.

What makes my approach unique is a combination of personal experience, practical tools, and deep empathy. I don't just hand you a plan and leave you to figure it out. I walk with you every step of the way, helping you rewrite the stories, holding you back and building habits that honor your worth. Together, we create a path that's as unique as you are.

THE COACHING CORNER

Affirmation:
- *I trust my abilities and embrace the infinite potential within me.*

Quote:
- *"Our deepest fear is not that we are inadequate. Our deepest fear is that we are powerful beyond measure." – Marianne Williamson*

Helping Others Break Free

Through trial and error, I began to see patterns emerge in my work. So many women struggled with saying no. They carried guilt for putting their needs first and felt stuck in stories that told them they weren't enough.

Robyn came to me feeling stuck and overwhelmed. She described her life as a constant battle between keeping everyone else happy and feeling utterly invisible. The idea of saying no terrified her. 'What if they stop liking me?' she asked.

Together, we worked on reframing her beliefs about worthiness. We started small, practicing scenarios where she could say no without overexplaining. The first time she did it, she said, 'I felt like a weight lifted off my shoulders.' From there, she began setting boundaries with confidence. Today, Robyn tells me she has more energy, stronger relationships, and, most importantly, a sense of freedom she never thought possible.

THE COACHING CORNER

The first time she told me, "I said no without guilt," my heart swelled with pride and gratitude. It wasn't just a small win—it was a life-changing shift for her. Moments like these remind me why I do this work.

Journal Prompts:

- *Can you think of a time you said yes when you wanted to say no? How would your life feel different if you had set a boundary instead? What would it feel like to say no in a similar situation next time?*

Another client, Sarah, struggled with balancing her career and personal life. She had convinced herself that saying no at work would make her seem unreliable, even though she was burning out. By challenging this belief and helping her set boundaries, Sarah not only reclaimed her energy but also received a promotion because her leadership team admired her confidence.

Journal Prompts:

- *What is one area of your life where burnout is holding you back? How might setting a boundary improve your energy or effectiveness?*

Sam's story offers a different perspective. As a business owner, she struggled to set boundaries with clients and colleagues. She constantly overexplained herself, seeking approval and validation. One simple question— "What if you don't owe them an explanation?" completely changed her mindset. Today, Sam runs

THE COACHING CORNER

her business with confidence, making decisions that align with her values and priorities.

Journal Prompts:
- *What is one area of your life where you've felt the need to overexplain yourself? What might happen if you simply said no instead?*
- *What is one belief you've held about yourself that may no longer serve you? How would your life change if you replaced it with a more empowering belief?*

Common Myths About Bliss

Before we dive into creating your own path to bliss, let's talk about what bliss isn't. Too often, people hold onto myths about joy and fulfillment that keep them stuck in self-doubt and hesitation. Here are two of the most common misconceptions I see:

1. **Myth**: Bliss Means Everything is Perfect
   Bliss isn't about perfection. It's about learning to find joy, calm, and confidence even in the face of life's challenges. It's knowing you have the tools to navigate what comes your way while staying true to yourself.
2. **Myth:** Setting Boundaries Will Push People Away
   One of the biggest fears my clients have is that setting boundaries will damage their relationships. But boundaries create clarity and mutual respect. When you show up for yourself, the right people in your life will show up for you, too.

THE COACHING CORNER

The Bliss Blueprint: Belief + Boundaries in Action

This process isn't just a coaching framework, it's a lifestyle.
Each step builds on the foundation of shifting limiting beliefs, empowering you to set boundaries that honor your worth and lead you to a life of bliss.

Step 1: Believe You Are Worthy

The first step is transforming your internal dialogue. Without belief, every action feels forced or empty. This step focuses on recognizing and rewriting limiting beliefs.

How to Shift Beliefs:

- Identify one belief holding you back (e.g., "I'm not good enough").
- Ask yourself: *Is this true*? What evidence do I have for or against it?
- Replace it with an empowering belief (e.g., "I am capable of growth and success").

Believing you are worthy is the hardest and most crucial step. I know how scary it can feel to challenge a belief that has defined you for years. But here's the truth: You are not your past. You are not the sum of other people's opinions.

Shifting your beliefs is like learning a new language—it takes practice, but it's worth it. One client told me she had spent her entire life thinking, 'I'm not good enough.' Through our work together, she replaced that belief with, 'I am capable and deserving.' Today, she says, 'I finally feel free."

Transform your internal dialogue by rewriting limiting beliefs.

- **Journal Prompts:** What is one belief about yourself that feels like a chain holding you back? How has this belief influenced your decisions? What evidence do you have that this belief might not be true?
- **Exercise:** Write down a belief you'd like to change. Underneath it, write three pieces of evidence that prove this belief isn't true.
- **Affirmation:** Every day, I grow more confident in my abilities and worth.

Step 2: Set Boundaries That Honor Your Beliefs

Once you believe you are worthy of joy and respect, boundaries become an act of self-love. This step is about learning to say no to what drains you and yes to what aligns with your values.

How to Shift Beliefs:

- Reflect on the fear behind your lack of boundaries. Do you believe saying no makes you selfish or unkind?
- Replace that belief with: "Saying no creates space for what truly matters."

THE COACHING CORNER

Example: A client of mine realized her reluctance to set boundaries stemmed from the belief that her value came from pleasing others. Once she shifted to believing her value was intrinsic, she began setting boundaries unapologetically.

Your value isn't determined by others. When you respect yourself and set boundaries, you teach others to respect you as well. On the other hand, allowing others to walk over you only perpetuates that dynamic. Which feels better: being respected or being overlooked?

Learn to say no without guilt and yes to what matters most.

- **Journal Prompts:** What's one area of your life where you feel overextended? What boundary could you set to reclaim your time and energy?
- **Exercise:** Practice a script to use to set this boundary. For example: If you are telling someone you can't do something, practice saying "Thank you for thinking of me, but that doesn't work for me this time." This lets them know you are open to future invites, and you are being kind by thanking them.
- **Affirmation:** My boundaries reflect my self-respect.

Step 3: Cultivate Harmony with Your New Beliefs

True balance comes from aligning your actions with your beliefs. This step focuses on creating routines and habits that reflect your worth and priorities.

THE COACHING CORNER

How to Shift Beliefs:

- Look at where your current habits contradict your desired beliefs (e.g., overworking despite valuing self-care).
- Ask yourself: What would someone who values themselves do in this situation?

Example: I once worked with a client who believed she had to sacrifice her needs to be a good mother. By shifting that belief, she created a weekly schedule that included guilt-free "me time," which made her a more present and joyful parent.

Align your actions with your values and priorities.

- **Journal Prompts:** Do your current routines reflect your priorities? If not, what is one habit you could change to better align with your values?
- **Exercise:** Create a daily self-care ritual that reinforces your worth, like taking five minutes each morning to list things you're grateful for.
- **Affirmation:** My actions align with my values and priorities.

Step 4: Embrace Bliss as a Practice

Bliss isn't a one-time achievement—it's a mindset. This step focuses
on celebrating progress, staying aligned with your beliefs, and continuing to refine your boundaries as life evolves.

THE COACHING CORNER

How to Shift Beliefs:

- Replace perfectionist beliefs (e.g., "I can't celebrate until I've achieved everything") with: "Every step forward is worth celebrating."
- Keep a gratitude journal to reinforce the belief that joy is abundant.

Example: One of my clients shared that she had never celebrated her wins because she believed she didn't deserve to. Through our work, she began acknowledging her progress, which deepened her sense of fulfillment.

Celebrate your progress and refine your boundaries as life evolves.

- **Journal Prompts:** What is one small win you've achieved recently? How can you celebrate it to reinforce your progress? How does acknowledging it make you feel?
- **Affirmation:** Every step I take brings me closer to the life I desire.

What Does Bliss Look Like?

Imagine waking up each morning with a deep sense of calm, no longer feeling the weight of endless obligations or second-guessing your decisions. Picture yourself sipping your coffee or tea in peace, knowing that your day is aligned with your priorities—not someone else's demands.

THE COACHING CORNER

Journal Prompt:
- If you could design your perfect day, what would it include? How would you feel at the end of it?

Bliss looks like confidently saying no to what drains you and yes to what fuels your soul. It feels like walking into a room and no longer questioning whether you belong there, you know you do. It sounds like laughter with loved ones, the soft hum of contentment as you finally take that trip you've been dreaming about, or the quiet satisfaction of carving out time for yourself guilt-free.

Bliss is waking up with energy because you're no longer running on empty. It's the joy of seeing your relationships flourish because you've learned to communicate your needs with clarity and grace. It's creating a life where self-care isn't a luxury but a non-negotiable part of your routine, and where your worth isn't tied to anyone else's opinion.

When you embrace belief and boundaries, bliss becomes your natural state. It's not about perfection; it's about living with intention, savoring the small victories, and knowing that you're on a path that feels right for you.

For me, bliss looks like building a life where while my father was in his last days, I could be by his side, and where I could help my mother out with all the things that had to be done after he was gone. Bliss also looks like being able to travel more, spending more

THE COACHING CORNER

time with family and friends, going on adventures with my husband, and connecting with the things that truly light me up.

- **Affirmation:** Bliss is knowing, deep in your heart, that you are worthy of joy, success, and love!

Building a Blissful Future

My mission is to show women that they are worthy of everything they desire. Whether it's setting a boundary for the first time or rewriting a belief that's been holding them back for years, every small step leads to big changes.

This journey isn't just about achieving a specific goal, it's about transforming the way you see yourself and your potential. It's about waking up each day with clarity, confidence, and a deep sense of joy, knowing you're in control of your story.

When you step into your worth and embrace bliss, the ripple effect is incredible. You inspire your children to set healthy boundaries, encourage your friends to prioritize themselves, and show your loved ones what's possible when you believe in yourself. Your transformation isn't just for you, it's for everyone whose life you touch.

I envision a future where women everywhere feel empowered to say no to what doesn't serve them and yes to their dreams. A future where self-worth isn't tied to external validation, but instead, to an unshakable belief in their value.

THE COACHING CORNER

What is one small step you can take today to rewrite a belief or set a boundary that honors your worth?

The road to bliss begins with one small step: believing it's possible. I encourage you to take a moment today to reflect on one belief that's been holding you back. Write it down, question its truth, and imagine what life could look like without it.

You're here because you know you're meant for more. You've already taken the first step by recognizing that something needs to change. Now it's time to take the next step—and I'm here to help. Whether it's rewriting a belief, setting your first boundary, or rediscovering your worth, you don't have to do it alone. Let's create your path to bliss together.

Journal Prompt:
- What is one limiting belief or unresolved boundary you can start working on today? What will taking that step mean for your future?

Connect with me:

Linktree: https://linktr.ee/thankfulheartscoaching
Website: https://www.thankfulheartscoaching.com/
Email: thankfulheartscoaching@gmail.com

THE COACHING CORNER

THE COACHING CORNER

Chapter 12

By Kelly Watts

Business Mentor, Marketing, and Launch Strategist

There must be more to life than this

One day, while sitting on the floor of an empty classroom with one of the SEN children I supported climbing over me, it struck me: surely there must be more to life than this?

I was working as a one-to-one TA (Teaching Assistant), dedicated to helping SEN children. I loved supporting them and celebrating their small but meaningful achievements. But as anyone who works in a school knows, it's exhausting.

On top of that, I was also a lunchtime supervisor, barely scraping above minimum wage, and then heading home to take on the role of Mum.

THE COACHING CORNER

Taking a holiday to recharge wasn't even a realistic option; it would take us years just to save enough. Rising living costs only underscored the question in my mind: what else could I do?

The obvious path was to retrain in another field, but that wasn't exactly practical. It meant sacrificing my school holidays, going without pay during those times, and taking on childcare costs before and after school for my son. Would any extra earnings even be worth it if they just went straight to childcare?

I was tired of working for other people, tired of feeling guilty whenever my son was unwell and I needed time off, tired of having to ask for permission to go on holiday. Why should we need someone else's approval to live our lives?

For eight years, I had raised my son alone. Now, in a relationship and sharing a home, I hoped that with two incomes, life might feel different. Yet, even with both of us working, the little luxuries still seemed out of reach.

I began to imagine what it might look like to work for myself, though I had no idea what that would entail. All I knew was that I wanted to be able to take my son on holiday. I wanted him to come home to a mum who wasn't worn out and irritable.

I was overwhelmed by work and the constant juggling act of home, hobbies, pets, appointments, and the general demands of life. Every day felt like just getting through, going to work to pay the bills, an existence on autopilot.

THE COACHING CORNER

Figuring out how I could step away from this, and create the life I was dreaming of, became the start of my journey into business.

Not enough hours in the day

Between work, school runs, late nights, and weekends, I felt like there were never enough hours in the day. Yet, I couldn't ignore the pull to learn more, to dive into every business course I could find. I made the most of every free moment—turning car rides, lunch breaks, and any spare minute into time for learning, determined to make a difference in our lives.

I've always loved learning, taking in new information, and putting it into practice. I remember when Oscar was a baby; even as a single mum, I completed a Higher Certificate in Education in Social Work (Wales). Back then, I was a social work assistant with ambitions to move forward. I planned to resit my Maths GCSE, as I needed a C grade or higher to continue in social work.

It was a harsh reminder of how restricted we can be by qualifications. Despite working as a social work assistant, my path to becoming a social worker was blocked by a grade. In the end, I didn't end up resitting my maths, but a few years later, I retrained as a teaching assistant alongside my social work role. I completed the course just as Oscar started school, allowing me to be there during half terms and avoid extra childcare as he grew.

Eventually, work-related stress led me to leave my council job after 11 years—right before the pandemic hit in March 2020. This isn't one of those COVID-era success stories; I didn't start a business then.

THE COACHING CORNER

I'm simply sharing the journey that brought me to each turning point.

When I finally decided I needed a big change, I threw myself into learning. Over the next few months, I spent every spare moment on HubSpot, OpenLearn, and FutureLearn, reading everything I could on business, branding, marketing, social media, and the online world. I still have notebooks filled with everything I learned!

At one point, it felt like my studies were taking over, and I became frustrated with the daily tasks that interrupted my learning. I knew I wanted out, and I knew that learning was my ticket. But with life so busy, there just weren't enough hours to absorb everything I needed.

Yes, I'm impatient—but only about the things I'm passionate about. It's a great strength when channelled correctly, but I was learning that this wasn't quite the right way.

I still can't believe this happened

I had been a single mum since Oscar was born, and at one point, I had to sell my house and move in with my aunt, Janet. As a single parent working part-time, it felt almost impossible to save enough for another house deposit, let alone manage a mortgage on my own, especially with rising property prices.

By January 2023, I had started feeling restless, thinking about a new path. I was determined to spend that summer creating an online business.

Just a few months before, in November 2022, my partner Dan, Oscar, and I had finally moved into our new home after living with my aunt for several years. I wonder now if this big change—having a place of our own—sparked something in me, a desire for more security, more independence.

But everything changed suddenly in February 2023. One day, I went to check in on my aunt, who had been unwell for a few days, and found that she had passed away in her bed. It was a massive shock—completely unexpected, especially as I had shared her home for years.

My focus immediately shifted as I processed my grief, took on the responsibility of arranging her funeral, managed her estate, and awaited the coroner's report, hoping for closure for our family.

The love had gone

I told myself I'd work in a school for just one more year before moving on. My passion for the job had faded I wanted freedom, the kind I knew I'd never find working for someone else.

Looking back, a year isn't much time to achieve something so ambitious, especially with no business background and no clear direction on what to learn first. But being stubborn, I wasn't going to let a lack of experience or time hold me back. I created a new Facebook account, and an Instagram profile, and began posting.

By the summer of 2023, I'd officially started my "online journey," even though I still didn't fully know where I was headed. I just had a gut

THE COACHING CORNER

feeling that others were in the same position as me, craving something different, and I wanted to help those who felt the same.

I began researching how to become a Virtual Assistant (VA), which kept popping up as a viable option. At this point, I still thought that not having a degree or high-level qualifications might limit my options.

I joined a weekly online challenge, which I now realise was a "boot camp," and started completing the free tasks it offered. Naturally, at the end came the big sales pitch for a pricey programme. At the time, the cost seemed overwhelming, and I wasn't ready to invest in something I'd only just started exploring. Determined to make it on my own, I was set on learning everything without the high costs.

I managed to learn quite a bit, but without structured guidance, it felt like trying to complete a black-and-white puzzle. I could piece together the edges, but I had no idea how to fill in the middle.

The six-week summer holiday flew by, with more time than I'd planned spent online. The weather was wet, which meant we stayed indoors a lot, leading me to dive even deeper into learning. Eventually, though, things began to click. I started to understand processes and learned what steps I needed to take to grow a business. Slowly but surely, I was piecing together a clearer picture of the path ahead.

One step forward ten steps back

As I navigated the early stages of building a business, I quickly realised that many foundational steps should have been set up from the beginning. This discovery was often frustrating—I'd think I was making progress, only to realise I was doing things out of order or skipping crucial steps entirely.

Some of these basics included defining my niche, conducting market research, identifying my ideal client, and creating lead magnets. Yes, all the essentials! But without any prior business experience, I didn't know where to start. The more I studied and read, the more these pieces started coming together, like slowly assembling a jigsaw puzzle.

At that point, I had barely managed to outline the edges of my puzzle, and even then, I kept double-checking to make sure each piece was in the right place.

In my eagerness to leave my current job, I pushed forward at full speed, hoping that the faster I learned and the more I posted, the sooner paying clients would follow. I was laser-focused on my end goal: leaving by the following summer.

Once I began learning the essentials for business success, I started applying them. These steps were crucial for lead generation, visibility, and creating content that showcased my offers. But I still lacked a cohesive strategy—no in-depth research, no clear outcomes, and no real plan.

Then I came across a coach who was talking about sales. I knew that sales were at the heart of every business, yet no one else seemed to discuss it. Intrigued, I decided to work with this

THE COACHING CORNER

coach, visibility, mindset, setting goals, crafting offers, and targeting my ideal clients.

This was the turning point. I finally understood the power of visibility—and how essential it is for a business to thrive.

I built my business in the car!

When I was told to "get visible," I took it to heart—and took it up a notch. My time was limited with a young son, a full-time job, and evenings filled with trips to different hobbies. Add in a partner, two dogs, managing the house, and the usual life admin like medical appointments, and life was full-on.

I had to find gaps in my day to create content and make myself known for my "thing"—even though I still wasn't entirely sure what that "thing" was! So, I started looking for those little pockets of time. Evenings were already packed with endless scrolling, trying to learn everything I thought I needed (in hindsight, a lot of it was unnecessary!). Mornings, though, held potential. My partner left early, so instead of lying in bed, I started getting up at 6:30 a.m.

That extra hour was golden. I used it to connect on LinkedIn and Instagram, commenting on posts and building relationships. I recorded quick videos and shared how I managed my business around the morning school run. Soon, I took my filming to the car, and that's when things really took off.

I realised I was spending so much time sitting in the car, waiting.

THE COACHING CORNER

Ten minutes early for the school pick-up—not enough time to go home. Ten minutes after Oscar got on the school bus before I had to drive to work. Waiting outside his hobbies. Even before and after my taekwondo classes, or when I was early for my own black belt training (I'm a third dan, training for my fourth—fun fact!).

These "car moments" became my productivity pockets. I filmed videos, went live, connected with my ideal clients, left comments, and built relationships—all from the driver's seat.

The drive to leave my job kept me going, and I refused to let a lack of time be an excuse. Instead, I used it as fuel, a reminder that staying in my day job would only drain me further. I was already exhausted, and I knew I had to keep pushing if I wanted to break free.

In July 2024, just as I'd promised myself, I left my job at the school and stepped fully into my business.

Year 1: The First Lesson

My first year in business was a crash course in learning things the hard way! I felt like I was working backwards, figuring out the steps after I'd already taken them. But every bit of time and money I invested in myself, and my business taught me valuable lessons that got me to where I am today.

I'm now about to become a certified Launch & Marketing Strategist, and I'm also completing a certification in Mindset.

THE COACHING CORNER

Recently, I pivoted in my business, starting from scratch—this time with a solid foundation built on everything I've learned.

I've poured so much research into understanding my ideal client, and I now know how to conduct market research that truly gets results. This is how I help my clients today. When I started, I wanted to help others find the freedom to leave their jobs. Now, I do that through the tools, strategies, and techniques I've gained from the courses I've invested in and the experiences I've had.

Year one was an intense learning curve as a mum, a partner, and a business owner. I made plenty of mistakes but didn't give up. For someone with no business background, I consider it a successful year! Now, in Year 2, I'm using everything I learned to grow not just my own business but also those of my clients.

Want to know how to grow a business? Start with the essentials: understanding market research, defining your niche, and identifying your ideal client. You should aim to sell out your offers even before your course is created, all underpinned by a solid strategy. This is where I come in—I help new business owners, or those early in their journey, avoid the struggles I went through.

If you start with the right processes, stay committed, and remember that success doesn't happen overnight, you'll build a sustainable, successful business. Yes, there will be roadblocks; everyone faces them. That's why having a clear "Why" is essential. Your goals need to be bigger than just sales—they need to be the reason you keep going on tough days.

My Why? My son, Oscar. I wanted to create more time freedom for us, to be a more present, less frazzled mum. I wanted financial freedom so that we could book a holiday, go on adventures, or say "yes" to experiences without worrying about money.

So, there it is: the journey of an ordinary working mum with no business background, just a dream and the determination to make it happen. I even became a #1 bestselling author on the way to the school run one morning, with half-wet hair and before my first cup of tea!

My best advice? Just start today.

Work with Me to Build Your Own Success Story

Ready to launch and grow your coaching business but feeling unsure where to start? You don't have to go it alone. I specialise in helping new coaches build thriving, successful businesses from the ground up. Whether you're just starting out, pivoting, or feeling stuck, I'll guide you through each step so you can turn your passion into a reality. Here's what we'll work on together:

Crafting Your Unique Marketing Strategy: Together, we'll develop a strategic and authentic approach to connect with your ideal clients.

Client Acquisition: I'll help you build streamlined, effective processes to attract, engage, and retain clients—without the overwhelm.

THE COACHING CORNER

Establishing a Strong Business Foundation: From defining your niche to setting your pricing, we'll create a solid groundwork for long-term success.

Don't wait to launch the business and life you've been dreaming of. Reach out, and let's start building the path to your coaching success. Your journey to making an impact and helping others begins now—let's make it happen, together!

Contact me

Linktree https://linktr.ee/kelly3011

THE COACHING CORNER

Chapter 13

Manifesting a Life You Love:

The Journey from Survival to Limitless

By Heather Rosewood

My Background and Journey

For years, I lived a life shaped by abandonment and insecurity. Growing up in a household with divorced parents, I was constantly craving love or affection that just wasn't available. It wasn't that my parents didn't love me; nothing could be further from the truth. My parents didn't know how to love. They were products of their upbringing. It was a pattern. Growing up this way instilled a deep-seated fear of rejection that would echo throughout my life, influencing my choices and relationships. Growing up, I was insecure, never learning how to give or receive love. I became a people pleaser. I was always putting everyone

THE COACHING CORNER

else's needs above mine in a desperate attempt to gain approval and avoid the pain of being abandoned again. If they needed me, they would keep me.

The impact of my childhood experiences was profound. I navigated relationships and life decisions through a lens of anxiety and uncertainty. My sense of self-worth was intricately tied to the validation I received from others. When I got married, I thought I had found stability, but I soon realized that was not the case. I could not see the signs, but the mental abuse was real. Being told I was worthless and disgusting played right into my already insecure identity. I felt trapped, unable to assert my needs or desires for fear of creating conflict or being rejected.

After a brutal divorce that shattered my world, I found myself at rock bottom with two little girls to care for. I was emotionally broken, consumed by self-doubt and negative thoughts, often speaking to myself in ways I would never dream of saying to anyone else. The echoes of my past replayed in my mind, "You're not enough. You'll always be left behind." It was a painful cycle that left me feeling lost and hopeless.

I was faced with a choice. Do I continue living in fear, or should I find a way out of the darkness? Deep down, I knew that I didn't want my daughters to grow up witnessing a mother who felt powerless. I felt lost, scared, and hopeless, but I wasn't about to let that be their childhood story. I went from being a stay-at-home mom to depressed and hopeless, renting a room from my aunt and trying to figure out how to support two little girls. I knew I had to figure it out, and failure was out of the question.

I searched frantically for ways to make money quickly so I could pay the bills and invest in myself because, like many of you, there was something in me that knew my life was meant for more. I just didn't know what it was or how to go about finding it. So I borrowed the money for supplies and started a small jewelry business. I was determined to show them that it was possible to be successful if you worked hard enough if you wanted it bad enough.

I stumbled upon the Law of Attraction and manifestation by what I thought was an accident. I approached the concept with skepticism, unsure if it was real or a bunch of, 'woo woo fairy tales.' Could this truly make a difference in my life? But as I went deeper into the principles of manifestation, something was shifting in my beliefs and subconscious. I realized that I had the power to change my circumstances—not just by wishing for a better life but by actively taking steps toward creating it.

I started by writing down my dreams and desires, not just related to money but also about discovering my true passion and purpose. I worked hard to figure out who I actually was. My whole life, I lived other people's dreams and hobbies. I visualized my ideal life—what it looked like, how it felt, and how it would impact me and everyone around me. I envisioned a life filled with joy, abundance, and fulfillment. I saw myself breaking free from the loneliness and abandonment that had been my story for so long.

THE COACHING CORNER

I started seeing little changes, to begin with, but they were enough to make me believe in this. I doubled down on my new mindset and began to take inspired action. I signed up for courses, networked with like-minded individuals, hired a coach, and immersed myself in personal development. Each small step reinforced my belief in my ability to create the life I dreamed of. The shift from survival mode to living fully was not immediate, but it was profound.

I embraced an abundance mindset, celebrating every small victory along the way. From making necklaces on my kitchen table to flying first class and buying my dream house, each accomplishment was a testament to my journey of self-discovery and empowerment. This experience taught me that manifestation isn't just about wishing for things; it's about believing in yourself and taking the inspired action necessary to achieve your dreams.

Today, I am a Personal Development Manifestation Coach. I am passionate about helping as many people as possible through this work.

The Three Planes

With my understanding of manifestation and personal growth, I developed a holistic approach I now share with my clients. I believe that manifestation is a combination of spirituality and personal growth and development. I rearrange the popular phrase "mind, body, spirit" to "spirit, mind, body." In my experience, that is the order it should be in. These represent the three planes we live in, the Spiritual Plane, The Intellectual Plane, and The Physical Plane.

THE COACHING CORNER

My process involves several key components that help clients align their thoughts, feelings, and actions with their desires.

I integrate insights from top experts to explain how manifestation works. For instance, concepts like neuroplasticity help illustrate how our thoughts can reshape our reality by forming new neural pathways. By providing this scientific foundation, I empower clients to understand that they can create change through their thoughts and emotions.

I strongly emphasize building a supportive community for my clients. I believe that when people feel supported and understood, there is no limit to what they can do. Through my online programs, meetups, and retreats, I create safe spaces for clients to share their journeys and learn from one another, fostering a sense of belonging and collective growth.

While many coaches discuss manifestation in terms of desire, I emphasize the importance of cultivating an abundance mindset and practicing gratitude. Shifting focus from lack to abundance is vital for attracting what you want in life This perspective not only helps clients manifest their goals but also plants a deeper sense of fulfillment and joy in their daily lives.

Here are some actionable steps you can use now.

The first step I teach is helping my clients understand where they are now. If you don't know where you are, you can't know where you are going. When I was learning this material, it was shifting the narrative in my mind, replacing doubt with love. This shift in thinking

THE COACHING CORNER

required embodying the material. I had to learn to be kind to myself, to fall in love with the woman I was right then.

Many people carry subconscious beliefs that sabotage their efforts to manifest. I use cognitive restructuring and visualizations to help clients reframe their thoughts and see where they are.

Through journaling and visualization practices, I focused on the life I desired rather than the limitations I had experienced. I envisioned myself thriving—traveling the world, owning my dream house, and enjoying financial freedom. Each time I envisioned this life, I felt the energy and excitement. I began to understand that manifestation was not just about wishful thinking; it was about embodying the feelings and energy of the life I wanted.

This is where the spirit part comes in. Once you are aware of your starting point, you will find your spiritual awareness. Whatever this is for you, visualizations, walking in nature, journaling, meditation, whatever connects you spiritually to source energy. You can call it source, the universe, God; it doesn't matter what you call it; it's a feeling.

Feel the connection you have to your source energy. We have to make sure there is space for us to receive, to have intention, and to understand the power of our thoughts. We guide and direct source energy with our thoughts, feelings, and actions. You can't do that if you aren't connected to source energy.

Now we move into the intellectual part, the mind. This is where we ask ourselves what we want. This is what we will write down, create

THE COACHING CORNER

a scene, and put on a vision board. What does the elevated version of you want? This is the fun part, where we use our imagination and create any and everything our heart desires. This is where we create the elevated version of ourselves.

What do you need to do to be next level you? If you are a procrastinator, constantly judging, or live for gossip, this is where your self-awareness will come full circle. You can pick the things you love about yourself and the things you want to change and create your new identity in the intellectual plane: your new identity, the one where you are worthy and confident. We are here today because I chose to believe in myself. Remember that you can't expect change doing the same thing, so you can't expect next level you without changing how you think and show up for yourself. Once you have created this new identity, it's time for the physical plane. It is time to show up as who you need to be for next level you. This means taking action. Saying you are going to do it and actually doing it are not the same thing, if you show up dressed, talking, and acting like next level you, everyone will treat you as next level you. This is not a fake it til you make it moment. This is you taking action and actively changing your vibration to match who next level you are. Believing that it is already here, it is done. The more you show up as next level you, the more you become the identity you created.

Manifestation is not solely about positive thinking; it requires action. I emphasize the importance of taking inspired action toward one's goals. We explore practical steps my clients can take

THE COACHING CORNER

to align their efforts with their intentions, creating a momentum propelling them forward.

Throughout the process, I celebrate abundance, mindset, and next-level you. This includes practicing gratitude, celebrating small wins, and visualizing success regularly. I encourage my clients to surround themselves with positive influences and create an environment that supports their growth.

By integrating these elements into my coaching, I empower individuals to manifest their dreams and create lives filled with purpose and abundance. Each lesson is tailored to meet the unique needs of my clients, providing them with the tools and strategies necessary to navigate their journeys successfully.

I teach my clients the steps I still use in my life every day. We practice gratitude actively.

Gratitude helped me keep a mindset of appreciation, allowing me to attract even more positive experiences. As I celebrated my victories, I opened the door to greater abundance.

I also found solace in meditation, using it as a tool to quiet my mind and connect with my source energy. During these moments of stillness, I could hear my intuition guiding me toward my dreams. I learned to trust that voice and allow it to lead me, reinforcing my belief that I was on the right path. Meditation doesn't have to be sitting still in a room, and it can take on many forms, hiking and going for walks are among my favorites. Time in nature helps me reconnect with my purpose.

THE COACHING CORNER

As I deepened my practice, I discovered that self-discovery is a vital part of the manifestation process. Understanding my core values, passions, and strengths allowed me to align my goals with my true self. The more I connected with who I was, the easier it became to manifest the life I desired.

Transformational Success Stories

What inspired me to start teaching this material and become involved in the manifestation coaching industry was my own transformation. I realized that many people struggle with limiting beliefs and self-awareness, which can block their paths to success and fulfillment. My mission became clear: I wanted to empower others to embrace their potential and transform their lives through the same practices that had worked for me. I've been there to walk the walk and talk the talk.

What truly drives me is witnessing my clients' transformations. It is incredibly rewarding to see them overcome their fears, break free from limiting beliefs, and manifest their dreams. I believe that everyone can create the life they desire, and it's my passion to guide them on that journey.

What sets me apart from others in the manifestation coaching industry is my holistic approach, which combines practical techniques with deep self-discovery—science meets woo-woo, if you will. While many coaches focus solely on the surface-level aspects of manifestation, such as affirmations or visualization, I emphasize the importance of understanding one's core beliefs and

THE COACHING CORNER

emotional patterns.

One of my clients, a single mother struggling to do it all, went from being stressed and feeling inadequate to thriving by embracing the principles of manifestation. Through our coaching sessions, she learned to shift her mindset and implement practical manifestation techniques. I guided her to visualize her goals and practice gratitude daily. Within months, she had started the business she had always dreamt of and is now a very successful entrepreneur.

Another client came to me feeling lost and unfulfilled in her career. After spending years in a job that drained her energy, she felt too afraid to make a change. We worked together to uncover her passions and set clear intentions for her future. By the end of our sessions, she had successfully transitioned to a career in coaching that aligned with her true self, reigniting her passion for life. Her transformation was remarkable, and she now encourages others to embrace their authentic selves.

Your Journey Awaits

No matter where you are in life, you can create the reality you desire. The Law of Attraction is a tool that, when used correctly, can help you unlock abundance and manifest your dreams.

I encourage you to take the steps toward what you truly want in life. What are your dreams? What does your ideal reality look like? Embrace the feelings that come with those desires and allow them to guide your thoughts and actions.

THE COACHING CORNER

It's essential to cultivate a mindset of abundance and gratitude. Begin by acknowledging the blessings in your life, no matter how small. Create a gratitude journal where you can jot down your thoughts and feelings. This practice will shift your focus, making it easier to attract what you truly desire.

Remember, changing your thoughts is the first step toward changing your life. Surround yourself with positivity, practice self-love, and never underestimate the power of your mind. Your manifestation journey is waiting for you, and I am here to support you every step of the way.

How Can I be of Service?

If you're ready to take the next step on your manifestation journey, I invite you to explore the programs available through **The Rosewood Academy.** We provide a range of programs, from one-on-one coaching sessions to online courses, all designed to empower you to manifest your dreams. We also have a private membership community aptly named The Manifesting Society, where we offer an active community, guest coaches, workshops, and so much more.

In my coaching, we will work together to uncover your unique path, identify and overcome limiting beliefs, and develop a clear roadmap for achieving your goals. My goal is to equip you with the tools and strategies necessary for success, fostering a sense of confidence and empowerment along the way.

THE COACHING CORNER

Join me in creating a life filled with abundance, purpose, and fulfillment. Your journey to manifesting the life you love is just a step away. Let's embark on this transformative adventure together.

Big Love,

Heather

Linktree: https://linktr.ee/heatherrosewood

Website: www.heatherrosewood.com

Facebook: www.facebook.com/iamheatherrosewood

YouTube: www.youtube.com/@IamHeatherRosewood

Instagram: www.instagram.com/iamheatherrosewood/

TikTok: www.tiktok.com/@iamheatherrosewood?_t=8rJ01WSpm4A&_r=1

THE COACHING CORNER

Chapter 14

By Sarah Luke

Learning designer & facilitator and Coach

Roots of the Rainforest

Curious by design and curious by nature, I bring my fascination with people into everything I do. With over 19 years of experience in Learning and Development, and 10 years in coaching, I have worked across a variety of sectors as both an internal facilitator and an independent consultant, helping teams and individuals grow. As a facilitator and coach, I bring energy and authenticity to every session, empowering people to learn, explore, and take charge of their personal development.

Let me take you back to where it all began.

THE COACHING CORNER

I grew up in a vibrant, mixed heritage home in North West London as the eldest of three children. My street was as colourful and diverse as a rainforest canopy, full of inviting neighbours who opened their homes, shared their cultures, and treated us to delicious home-cooked meals.

I look at my upbringing with wonder now, my mum raised me speaking her native Swiss-German and my father shared all the wonderfulness of his Bangladeshi roots, and a lot of my early years was spent with my Scottish friend Dean and his family, where I picked up their Glaswegian accent. You can picture it now - a mixed-race five-year-old, with a Swiss mum, a Bangladeshi dad, and a thick Scottish accent starting school!

This diverse upbringing shaped my curiosity about people, their stories, and the unique qualities that make us who we are. It taught me to listen, adapt, and embrace different perspectives—skills that naturally led me to a career in learning, development and coaching.

Emerging Through the Undergrowth

Like many people, my early career was a journey of trial and error. Moving from one job to the next, I learned what I enjoyed, where my strengths lay, and what I needed to change. Along the way I experienced both supportive mentors and challenging managers. While I sought roles that aligned with my values, I often found that company values didn't always translate into the individual behaviours of my managers.

I noticed that my experiences at work were repeating themselves, even though I thought I had found new and better opportunities. I'd leave one role hoping to find something better, only to face similar or different challenges in the next.

What I didn't realise at the time was that the common thread wasn't the jobs, the bosses, or the colleagues—it was my own mindset and beliefs.

I was holding on to past experiences seeing them only through my own lens. These perceptions validated my thoughts and shaped my feelings, which in turn drove behaviours that, at best, weren't always helpful, and at worst, were self-destructive. For example, one boss I had repeatedly labelled me as forgetful and inefficient, and I internalised this to become my own narrative, doubting my abilities. Another manager who didn't share their thoughts, didn't seek my opinions or ask for my ideas made me become overly defensive.

These thoughts and feelings led me to make decisions or act in ways that weren't useful for any of us – for me, my managers at the time or our colleagues. It perpetuated the situations, resulting in me losing a lot of confidence or looking for opportunities to find fault and blame others for what was happening. In short, I was limiting my chances of moving forward or achieving what was

THE COACHING CORNER

possible for me.

It was only later, through studying the Cognitive Behavioural Model during my master's program and my work as a coach, that I understood the cycle I was trapped in. The model revealed how our thoughts, feelings, and behaviours are interconnected and how we can break that cycle to create more empowering outcomes. I met people from different organisations, and listened to their experiences of the world of work, and their relationships with clients, colleagues and senior leaders.

As my fellow Masters and Coaching colleagues shared stories with me, I could relate them to my own experiences. I began coaching and many of my clients explained how they felt stuck and struggled to move forward or procrastinated.

Across my network of colleagues and coaching clients, I could see common themes. I found our choices, our decisions, and the way we reacted to situations were a result of only one side of the story. The side we chose to see. It became clear that I, and others I had spoken to or coached, found ourselves in situations that influenced the way we thought or felt and consequently how we then reacted – either in our communication, the decisions we made, or the actions we took.

The Cognitive Behavioural Model helped me understand and put context to what was being experienced. The image below indicates the interrelationships I describe above and how they influence each other.

```
                      Feelings
                       ↗    ↘
Situation ⟶ Thoughts         Behaviours ⟶ Outcome
                       ↘    ↗
                      Physical
                      reactions
```

The Cognitive Behavioural Model above is taken from a clinical setting and draws on the work of researchers and psychologists like Aaron Beck and Albert Ellis. In coaching, the application is adapted, and the benefits allow us to break down a situation and self-evaluate each component and how they relate, helping us realise the impact and what we can do to change the end outcome so that it serves us better.

Over time, reading and researching this approach and its application in coaching helped me understand how I was using my own thoughts, beliefs and feelings to perpetuate my behaviours that were ultimately counterproductive.

Weaving Our Way Amongst the Canopy

Allow me to help you better understand how I and other coaches, use Cognitive Behavioural Coaching (CBC) and find it beneficial for our clients. Let's begin with the terminology. The term 'cognitive'

THE COACHING CORNER

refers to our thoughts, memories, and attention, while 'behavioural' focuses on what we do and how we respond. Coaching, meanwhile, is about listening deeply and asking powerful questions that enable clients to discover their own solutions. Coaching empowers the individual to discover their own solutions to their challenges or limiting beliefs, allowing them to enhance their performance or achieve their goals. I'll explain my coaching approaches in more detail in part four.

There are many benefits to using CBC in coaching and I use this approach fluidly alongside other coaching models where appropriate. My coaching clients often complete the coaching with a stronger sense of self-awareness, problem-solving skills, and a toolkit for managing future challenges. In using CBC my clients grow in confidence, making the process of motivating themselves much easier. My coaching clients recognise and always reinforce that the coaching has promoted new thoughts and ideas that help change their behaviours and mindsets. The simplicity of CBC makes it easy for clients to adopt and practice self-coaching, fostering independence and resilience.

CBC is rooted in the idea that our reactions are the result, and stem not directly from the situations themselves, but from *our beliefs or interpretations of them.*

Through CBC, I help clients focus on the present to define their desired future. During the coaching conversation, I will listen out for keywords or phrases that define what they think or feel, examining

THE COACHING CORNER

their assumptions, challenging the evidence supporting their beliefs, and exploring alternative perspectives. I help my clients unpick these assumptions, beliefs and perspectives, allowing them to check if they are reasonable or can be justified, and explore facts or interpretations that may be contributing to the self-perceived challenges. It's at this point that the magic of self-awareness happens, and my clients may find their interpretations are often misguided or inaccurate. As a coach it's important I listen, not just to the words being said but also to what isn't being said. I ask questions that allow my coaching client to stay in that space, and their interpretation of what's happening. I use questions that probe my clients' conceptual understanding of the situation, that probe their assumptions and the reasons and evidence for that belief or thought.

The coaching process then takes a different turn, and we shift to reframing or changing mindsets and empowering my clients to take purposeful action. The questions continue to allow the client to move forward. This can involve self-learning from the insights the client makes or trying out new ways of thinking and feeling. I encourage my coaching clients to try out different narratives from the thoughts that interfere with their goals to ones that enhance the progress towards their goals. This is not a quick process. It is a step-by-step approach that helps individuals take control of the situation, and how the situation can be influenced by *changing their thoughts, beliefs, and feelings*.

THE COACHING CORNER

Take a moment to consider your own example. Think about a time when you found yourself in a difficult or uncomfortable situation or where you have talked yourself out of doing something. Perhaps you convinced yourself that you can't achieve something. Those limiting beliefs or negative thoughts consequently influence how you feel and your emotions that follow, for example, hurt, anger, and frustration. We can become self-defeatist. I shouldn't have defined myself by the labels my boss used in front of me, but I allowed her words, and her view to become my own story. Those thoughts made me doubt myself and feel inadequate. Those frustrations created by my self-doubt turned into something far less productive, making me trip up doing everyday tasks.

Apply cognitive behavioural coaching to your own example, allow yourself to explore alternative viewpoints, and change your negative beliefs around what you are feeling. Seek different ways of feeling and alter your response and actions. This in turn should help you reach possibilities of what you are capable of rather than the limits within which you are restricting yourself to. Cognitive behavioural coaching allows us to bring curiosity into the conversation. If we can talk ourselves into ineffectiveness, surely we are also able to talk ourselves out of it. *It's all about finding an alternative narrative.*

The Sunlight Beyond

I say it a lot to friends and colleagues, I really do enjoy coaching. Over time I have opened up to different perspectives of coaching

THE COACHING CORNER

and understand when I need to take different approaches. After all, coaching is the most successful when we respond to our clients, tailoring the way we coach to best meet the style and needs of the people or teams needing our support. Coaching can take on many forms from the more directive approach, perfect for those wanting to master a skill and often used in sport, or guided coaching which moves more to the direction of support whilst still allowing the client to reflect. Moving along further, towards pure coaching which, in contrast to directive coaching, is all about self-awareness, clarity from within and space to grow and learn at one's own pace.

Wanting to help others comes naturally to me and I learnt quickly that needing to adapt my coaching would be the common differentiator between my wish to help and my clients being able to achieve what they wanted from my coaching. I love being an inspiration to my clients through the power of coaching, noticing how proud my clients are of their own transformation as they progress through the coaching.

There are many of my coaching clients that have really touched my heart because their stories could have been my own or their journeys resonated with me. To be able to demonstrate the transformative power of coaching, however, I feel it is best illustrated through sharing stories.

One client I worked with was a young professional navigating the challenges of dyslexia in the workplace. He spent hours over-

THE COACHING CORNER

preparing and double-checking his work, consumed by a fear of being judged. He asked me to be his coach, helping him find ways or strategies to "workaround" his dyslexia. As we began the coaching, he shared how he had allowed the negativity he had experienced growing up as a child with dyslexia to shape his inhibitions at work. These inhibitions turned into feeling anxious, spending many hours after the working day, going over work, rewriting documentation, and worrying that colleagues and clients would pick up on his mistakes. We identified and reframed the negative beliefs he had internalized since childhood. By focusing on and isolating the negative thoughts and beliefs, it became possible *to* **utilise alternative viewpoints and behaviours to ultimately alter and reframe his outlook.** These alternative viewpoints and behaviours, in turn, reinforced by positive feedback from his manager and colleagues, created a **'new self'** by discarding his old beliefs. When we started coaching, I asked him what he *really wanted*. His answer was "a girlfriend" because he wasn't allowing himself any free time to enjoy it with friends. I saw him a year after the coaching finished and he beamed at me with a big smile. How are you? I asked. "I have a girlfriend"! he exclaimed. I was so proud that he no longer defined himself by his dyslexia.

Another client I coached, was a team leader who started work after a career break to care for her children. She felt hugely grateful for the opportunity to work flexibly in a senior role. She felt very privileged to have acquired such a position that allowed her to lead on projects and be able to work it around her home commitments. A short while into her new role however she was struggling with her Senior Leader with whom she often found herself in conflict. After a few months she came to me to request coaching. We uncovered her belief that her leader's indecisiveness would stall the projects she was leading. Using the Myers-Briggs Type Indicator, (MBTI), a personality tool that helps people understand their choices and preferences, this tool helped provide alternative perspectives. She had twisted herself up in knots and by the time she had sought my help in coaching she had become so confused as to what was true and what was her own concoction of events. When used in conjunction with CBC, the MBTI tool helped my client identify where she may have been allowing her preferred style to dominate, potentially limiting more effective approaches to resolving the issues she was facing.

Cognitive behavioural coaching allowed us to explore and experiment with more collaborative approaches, reframing her perspectives of her senior leader. In our final coaching session, she was almost in tears as she confessed that she felt coaching was the last option before possibly quitting her job which she desperately didn't want to do. She was so glad she went through with the coaching claiming it had resolved not just the relationship with her supervisor, but it had also renewed her self-confidence.

These moments reaffirm why I enjoy coaching so much. It's incredibly rewarding to help clients see new possibilities and rewrite

THE COACHING CORNER

their narratives. My hope is always that the impact I have has a ripple effect on my clients where they can adopt the CBC approach themselves with their team members or friends.

Thriving in the Ecosystem

Over the years as an independent consultant, I've been fortunate to work with some wonderful clients and well-known brands. Many of my clients come through referrals as I tend to prioritise securing positive and trust-based relationships with my clients over marketing myself through various mediums.

Across my business, the feedback my clients provide tends to follow a theme: that I take a tailored approach to everything I do, taking care that I understand the true nature of my clients' requirements. The way that I connect with my clients has stood the test of time and allowed me to receive referrals and recommendations. My approach is often described as genuine, personable, and empathetic and whether I am using tools like MBTI, TKI or Firo, or simply listening deeply, my aim is always to leave clients feeling inspired and confident. To quote one client, "You ensure that your feedback is constructive and easy to accept—balancing empathy with challenge". This blend of honesty and care seems to resonate with those I work with, especially for individuals who may otherwise find change difficult.

For me, coaching isn't just about achieving goals - I take pride in understanding the unique strengths, challenges, and dynamics of

THE COACHING CORNER

the people I support, it's about fostering long-term growth and resilience. My goal is to leave clients feeling inspired, equipped, and confident in their next steps. I've been described as intuitive and flexible, with an instinct for identifying exactly what is needed and adapting my coaching style to suit different personalities and goals.

It has been a privilege to help individuals and teams discover insights about themselves, deepen their understanding of others, and ultimately achieve meaningful and long-term results.

Do challenges or limiting beliefs hold you back from achieving your potential? Are you ready to discover the benefits and explore different perspectives, learning more about how your thoughts and feelings can positively impact your success?

I'd love to support you on your journey through cognitive behavioural coaching.

LinkedIn: linkedin.com/in/sarah-luke-9190805

Website: www.87consult.co.uk

THE COACHING CORNER

THE COACHING CORNER

Chapter 15

A Path to Wellness

By Noor Aishah

A Journey into Positive Psychology and Coaching

During my family's struggle with mental health in 2019, I found myself in unfamiliar territory. As a mother, I faced a situation many parents dread: my children were diagnosed with anxiety and depression. This news left me feeling lost and overwhelmed, uncertain of how to proceed.

The challenges did not end there. While striving to be a source of strength for my children, I found myself grappling with my own difficulties. Anxiety took hold, causing panic attacks that threatened my ability to support my family. It was during this personal and family crisis that I came to a crucial realisation: I could not effectively help my children if I did not first help myself.

THE COACHING CORNER

This insight sparked a life-changing journey. It would alter my life reshape my approach to parenting and lead me to another calling. In my search for solutions, I discovered the field of positive psychology. This approach was not just about treating illness; it was about fostering well-being. I recognised the opportunity to rediscover myself and enhance my family's approach to wellbeing.

Motivated by a newfound sense of purpose I pursued a Graduate Diploma in Applied Positive Psychology and a Graduate Diploma in Coaching Psychology from the School of Positive Psychology in Singapore. Each lesson was a step towards reclaiming my identity. I grew not just as a mother but as an individual with the capacity to grow and change.

As I applied these principles in my daily life, I began to observe significant shifts. I started celebrating small victories for anything that I am grateful for and approaching challenges with a growth mindset. The impact on my personal well-being was transformative. Even more rewarding was witnessing how these changes positively influenced the people around me.

This journey into positive psychology did more than alter my perspective. It gave me practical tools to address my family's challenges and ignited a passion for coaching and mental health advocacy. My belief that positive psychology and coaching can reshape lives drives me forward. My path from struggling parent to coach and advocate shows the potential for growth within us all.

This chapter invites you to explore how positive psychology can elevate lives. It presents a balanced view of mental health, emphasising that true well-being involves more than just the absence of illness—it is about nurturing positive mental states and flourishing. Whether you are a parent facing similar challenges or someone seeking to improve your own well-being, I hope my story and insights inspire and guide your own well-being journey.

Understanding Positive Psychology in Parenting

Positive psychology, founded by Martin Seligman, studies what helps people and communities thrive. Unlike traditional psychology that mainly focuses on fixing problems, positive psychology emphasises fostering flourishing. This field offers valuable insights for parents as they face the ups and downs of raising children. It encourages nurturing strengths in ourselves and our children. This approach focuses on cultivating positive emotions in family life. It also emphasises building resilience, rather than solely correcting negative behaviours. For parents, this shift in perspective can be eye-opening, providing new tools to support their children's well-being and their own.

At the core of positive psychology is the PERMA+H model, developed by Seligman and expanded by others in the field. This model identifies six key elements of well-being:

- **Positive Emotions (P)**
  Cultivating joy, gratitude, serenity, interest, hope, pride, amusement, inspiration, awe, and love.

THE COACHING CORNER

- **Engagement (E)**
  Fully immersing in activities, achieving a state of "flow."
- **Relationships (R)**
  Building and maintaining positive relationships.
- **Meaning (M)**
  Having a sense of purpose and feeling connected to something greater than oneself.
- **Accomplishment (A)**
  Pursuing success, achievement, and mastery for its own sake.
- **Health (H)**
  Maintaining physical and mental health through proper nutrition, exercise, and sleep habits.

Using the PERMA+H model in parenting does not mean we ignore problems. Instead, it helps us balance dealing with challenges while building a range of resources our children need to thrive long-term. These include mental, emotional, social, and physical resources. This approach gives us more tools than traditional parenting methods. It helps us not just solve problems but actively boost our children's well-being in all areas of their lives.

Unveiling VIA Character Strengths

The VIA (Values in Action) Character Strengths framework, developed by Christopher Peterson and Martin Seligman, is a powerful tool for personal growth and family well-being. It identifies 24-character strengths organised under six virtues:

- **Wisdom:** Creativity, Curiosity, Judgment, Love of Learning, Perspective
- **Courage:** Bravery, Perseverance, Honesty, Zest
- **Humanity:** Love, Kindness, Social Intelligence
- **Justice:** Teamwork, Fairness, Leadership
- **Temperance:** Forgiveness, Humility, Prudence, Self-Regulation
- **Transcendence:** Appreciation of Beauty, Gratitude, Hope, Humour, Spirituality

Character strengths are like special superpowers we all have inside us. They are different from talents or skills because they are part of who we are as people. These strengths are good qualities that everyone can grow and use in different parts of their lives, like at home, in school or with friends. People all around the world think these strengths are important and using them helps us feel happy and do well in life.

Nurturing character strengths in themselves and their children allows parents to set the stage for lifelong personal growth. Parents play a vital role in helping their children grow into caring and confident individuals. One powerful way to do this is by focusing on character strengths - both in themselves and in their children. This approach can transform family life and relationships in many positive ways.

When parents learn about their own natural strengths, they gain a better understanding of themselves. This self-awareness helps them interact more genuinely with their children and other family

THE COACHING CORNER

members. It also creates a special language for talking about what makes each person unique, which can bring the whole family closer together.

Using character strengths can make everyday family life more rewarding. When family members do activities that match their top strengths, they often feel happier and more satisfied. This increased engagement can make family time more enjoyable and meaningful for everyone.

Character strengths are also powerful tools for facing life's challenges. When families approach problems using their strengths, they often come up with more creative and effective solutions. This strength-based approach helps build resilience, making it easier for both parents and children to cope with stress and difficult times.

Perhaps the most beautiful outcome of focusing on character strengths is how it helps family members appreciate each other's differences. As parents and children learn about each person's unique mix of strengths, they start to value what makes everyone special. This creates a home environment where all family members feel understood and valued for who they are.

Inside the Positive Psychology Coaching Process

My approach to coaching is grounded in positive psychology principles, offering a comprehensive framework to support parents and children in their journey towards well-being and personal

THE COACHING CORNER

growth. This process is designed to be practical, focusing on building strengths and developing resilience.

I begin with a thorough initial assessment. The parent or child takes the VIA Character Strengths Survey to identify their top character strengths, providing a foundation for strength-based coaching. I conduct a comprehensive initial interview to explore the individual's current situation, challenges, and aspirations, with key questions focusing on areas such as life satisfaction, personal values, and moments of success. Beyond simply identifying strengths, we analyse how these strengths appear in daily life and where there might be opportunities for greater engagement.

The next step involves setting meaningful, achievable goals that align with the individual's values and strengths. I use an enhanced version of the SMART framework, incorporating elements of well-being and character strengths. Visualisation techniques like the "Best Possible Self" exercise help the parent or child envision and articulate their ideal future, fostering hope and motivation. I ensure that goals are in harmony with their core values, promoting a sense of authenticity and purpose.

The heart of the coaching process lies in helping the individual recognise and leverage their character strengths. The parent or child is guided to actively look for expressions of their top strengths in their daily behaviours and experiences. We explore how to apply signature strengths across various life domains - at home, in school or work and in relationships. We also discuss the potential overuse of strengths and develop strategies for moderation, ensuring a

THE COACHING CORNER

balanced approach to personal growth. Throughout the coaching process, I incorporate various evidence-based positive psychology interventions to guide the individual in applying their character.

Tailoring for Parents and Youths

My coaching journey tailors its approach to meet the unique needs of parents and young people. For parents, the focus is on developing positive parenting strategies that align with their individual strengths. To help manage parenting challenges, I guide parents in building resilience, and developing the mental and emotional strength needed to navigate the ups and downs of raising children. I also work on helping parents cultivate a belief in their own ability to learn and grow and teaching them how to instil this growth mindset in their children. Additionally, I assist parents in identifying their unique strengths and applying these to their parenting approach, creating a more authentic and effective parenting style. This comprehensive approach aims to empower parents and create a family dynamic where both parents and children can thrive and develop to their full potential.

When working with young people, the emphasis shifts to building self-esteem and confidence. I dedicate time to developing emotional intelligence and coping skills which are crucial for navigating the challenges of growing up. Together, we set and pursue meaningful goals and explore strategies for managing pressures. This holistic approach supports young people in their journey towards becoming resilient and confident individuals.

THE COACHING CORNER

In more challenging situations, particularly with young people who may be resistant to change, I employ a specialised technique called motivational interviewing. A key aspect of my method involves gently highlighting the discrepancy between current behaviours and the individual's broader life goals to encourage self-reflection. Rather than directly opposing resistance, I work to "roll with it," using it as a tool for exploration and growth. Throughout this process, I consistently support the individual's belief in their ability to change (self-efficacy) and maintain an optimistic outlook on the potential for positive transformation. This approach aims to foster intrinsic motivation for change, respecting the individual's autonomy while guiding them towards their aspirations.

Throughout our work together, I focus on three key areas: developing a "growth mindset" - the belief that one can learn and improve, celebrating small achievements along the way and continuously refining how we use individual strengths. My process involves regular check-ins to assess progress, setting achievable goals and using identified strengths to reach those goals.

This tailored blend of techniques addresses the complex dimensions of personal well-being. By combining various strategies, I create a customised plan that recognises and responds to the unique aspects of each individual's journey. This positive psychology-based coaching approach provides a robust toolkit for both parents and young people in their journey towards a more fulfilling and authentic life.

THE COACHING CORNER
Practical Tips for Positive Parenting

Integrating positive psychology into daily parenting can significantly enhance family well-being.

Here are evidence-based strategies to create a more positive family environment:

Identify and Nurture Character Strengths: Start by using the VIA Youth Survey to identify your children's top strengths. Once identified, make a conscious effort to regularly acknowledge when your children use these strengths. For example, if kindness is a top strength, praise your child when they share a toy or comfort a friend. Create challenges that allow children to apply their strengths in new ways, such as asking a child with the strength of creativity to help plan a family outing.

Practise Daily Gratitude: Implement a family gratitude ritual, like sharing three good things at weekly dinners. This simple practice can shift focus to the positive aspects of life. Encourage gratitude journalling, where children (and parents) write down things they are thankful for each day or each week. Model gratitude by expressing appreciation for everyday occurrences, like good weather or a delicious meal.

Foster a Growth Mindset: Praise effort and progress rather than fixed traits. Instead of saying "You're so smart," try "I'm impressed by how hard you worked on that problem." Reframe challenges as learning opportunities. When your child struggles with a task, encourage them to view it as a chance to grow. Involve children in problem-solving family challenges like planning a budget-friendly vacation. When your child faces a setback, help them analyse what went wrong and how they might approach it differently next time. Share stories of resilience from family history or role models to inspire and motivate.

Set and Pursue Meaningful Goals: Help children set age-appropriate, values-aligned goals. For younger children, this might be learning to tie shoelaces. For teenagers, it could be learning to manage their time more effectively. Break down goals into manageable steps and celebrate progress and effort, not just achievements. This approach teaches children the value of perseverance and the joy of gradual improvement. For instance, if a teen wants to improve his time management, discuss with him how he can set weekly goals like creating a study schedule, reducing social media use during homework time or completing assignments a day before they are due. Celebrate small wins such as finishing homework earlier or feeling less stressed about deadlines. This process not only helps them achieve better time management but also builds confidence and self-efficacy as they see themselves progressively gaining control over their daily routines.

Practise Positive Reframing: Guide children to find positive aspects in challenges. If a playdate is cancelled, help them see it as an opportunity for family time or to explore a new hobby. When a sports team loses a game, encourage focusing on the skills improved and lessons learned. Help reframe negative self-talk into

THE COACHING CORNER

balanced statements. For instance, change "I'm terrible at math" to "Math is challenging for me but I'm improving with practice" or "I'll never make friends at this new school" to "Making friends takes time and I can start by being friendly to one new person each day." Model positive reframing in your own life by verbalising how you find silver linings in difficult situations. For example, if stuck in traffic, you might say, "This gives us a chance to listen to another song" or if a work project does not go as planned, "This setback taught me valuable lessons for future projects." When we consistently practise this approach, children learn to develop resilience and a more optimistic outlook on life's challenges.

Promote Emotional Intelligence: Help children identify and name their emotions. Create a feelings chart with faces representing different emotions. Teach coping strategies for difficult emotions, such as deep breathing for anger or journalling for sadness. Validate feelings while guiding towards constructive responses. For example, "It's okay to feel angry but let's find a way to express it without hurting others."

Practise Self-Compassion: Model self-kindness when you make mistakes. If you burn dinner, instead of berating yourself, say "Cooking does not always go as planned. That's okay. We can make sandwiches instead." Encourage children to treat themselves with kindness, especially when they are struggling. Help children develop positive self-talk by teaching them phrases like 'I'm doing my best', 'Mistakes help me learn' or 'I can't do this yet but I will keep trying'. The word 'yet' is particularly powerful as it implies that skills and abilities can be developed over time with effort and practice.

Incorporating these principles builds a foundation for long-term well-being for both you and your children. Start small, be consistent, and adjust based on what works for your family. The goal is to create an environment where positive emotions, engagement, relationships, meaning, and accomplishment can flourish.

My Personal Journey: Transforming Fear into Action Through Positive Psychology Coaching

As both a recipient and practitioner of positive psychology coaching, I have witnessed firsthand its power to foster personal growth and professional development. Despite being an educator with more than 25 years of experience, I struggled with a deep-seated fear of public speaking. This fear stemmed from worries about being judged for my language and speaking ability, knowing that my anxiety often led to mistakes when addressing large audiences. This concern held me back from fully embracing opportunities to share my knowledge and make a broader impact.

Through coaching sessions, I gradually built the confidence needed to overcome this fear and take the crucial step of conducting workshops. A key aspect of this transformation was learning to differentiate between my roles – "taking off my Educator" hat and wearing "my advocacy mental health" hat. This shift in perspective significantly reduced my stress levels and

THE COACHING CORNER

allowed me to approach public speaking with renewed purpose.

Positive psychology coaching often involves exploring one's character strengths and values. In my case, becoming aware of my VIA strengths, particularly perseverance and love of learning, was instrumental. Recognising these strengths empowered me to leverage them in pursuit of my goals. I consistently sought out best practices for workshop delivery and used visualisation techniques to prepare, tapping into my natural inclination for continuous learning and persistence.

One particularly impactful exercise was writing my own eulogy. This reflective practice provided deep insights into how I wanted to be remembered, helping to shape my future actions and priorities. It illustrates how positive psychology interventions can increase self-awareness and clarify personal values.

These experiences solidified my belief in the power of positive psychology and coaching, motivating me to deepen my understanding and practice of these techniques.

Today, I conduct workshops on family resilience and positive psychology-related topics for the community – a goal I had set during my initial studies. This alignment between my work and innate capacities has increased my engagement, productivity, and sense of purpose.

I embrace the philosophy I share with others – I am not perfect, and that is okay. I am on a journey of continuous improvement. For example, I have not yet built the confidence to speak to a large audience in settings like halls or auditoriums. However, I view this not as a limitation but as an exciting opportunity for growth. I believe I will gradually develop this skill through practice and persistence. Just as I encourage others to use positive self-talk, I remind myself daily: "I may not be there yet, but I am making progress every day." This mindset keeps me motivated and helps me approach challenges with optimism and resilience.

Conclusion

The principles and practices I have explored offer a roadmap for creating more positive and nurturing family environments. As parents, by embracing positive psychology, you are equipping your children with tools to build resilience and improve wellbeing.

Start small but dream big. Begin with one or two practices that resonate with your family. Be consistent, patient and open to adjusting your approach. Remember, this is a journey of growth for everyone.

If you find yourself needing additional support or guidance in implementing these strategies, consider seeking the help of a positive psychology coach.

Thank you for joining this exploration of positive psychology in family life. Every step towards greater well-being creates ripple effects beyond yourself. The future of wellbeing is in our hands — let us co-create it together.

THE COACHING CORNER

About the Writer

Linktree: https://linktr.ee/savvyminds

Resources

For readers interested in exploring positive psychology further, here are some valuable online resources and titles of books that you may want to explore. It can provide you with a comprehensive understanding of the field and its potential for enhancing well-being and personal growth.

Website: https://savvyminds.weebly.com/positive-psychology-resources.html

THE COACHING CORNER

Chapter 16

Sculpting Success:

Transforming Work Through Intentional Design

By Ghazali Abdul Wahab

Navigating the Post-Pandemic World

The day Singapore announced its first COVID-19 case, I was sitting in my classroom, grading papers during lunch break. Little did I know that this news would trigger a chain of events that would completely transform my life and career as a teacher.

2020 started like any other year, but it quickly turned into something none of us had ever experienced before. As COVID-19 cases rose, our school, like many others across Singapore, had to adapt almost overnight. Suddenly, I found myself teaching through

THE COACHING CORNER

a computer screen, trying to keep twenty-five young faces engaged while dealing with technical difficulties, unmuted microphones and the constant worry that my students weren't really learning. The challenge was maintaining human connection in a world that felt increasingly distant and cold. Some of my students struggled with their home situations, others battled loneliness and a few simply disappeared from our virtual classroom despite our best efforts to reach them.

In the midst of all this chaos, I turned 45. Birthdays usually didn't bother me much, but something felt different this time. Maybe it was the isolation of lockdown or perhaps it was watching the news every night and seeing how fragile life could be. I started asking myself tough questions: What had I really achieved in my two decades of teaching? Had I made any real difference? Was I just going through the motions, or was there something more meaningful I could do with my life?

These questions kept me up at night. I'd lie in bed, thinking about all the dreams I had when I first started teaching. Dreams that somehow got buried under yearly schedules, endless marking and administrative tasks. The pandemic had stripped away all the usual distractions, forcing me to face these uncomfortable thoughts head-on. One particularly difficult night, after a frustrating day of frozen screens and disconnected students, I decided enough was enough. If this pandemic was teaching us anything, it was that life was too precious to waste on regrets. I started researching ways to find more meaning in my work, and that's when I stumbled upon the concept of job crafting in positive psychology.

The idea was simple but powerful: instead of changing jobs, you could reshape your current role to better match your strengths, values and passions. It was about making small, intentional changes that could add up to something meaningful.

What began as a mid-life crisis turned into something far more meaningful: a complete reinvention of my professional identity. Today, I work with adults and professionals, teaching them how to find deeper meaning in their work through job crafting. Every time I see someone's eyes light up as they realize they can reshape their work to better reflect their values and strengths, I'm reminded of my own journey of discovery. This is the reason I decided to explore being a career coach.

This is the story of how a crisis became a catalyst for transformation, not just for me, but for the countless professionals I now have the privilege to guide. Through job crafting, I didn't just find a new purpose; I found a way to help others discover theirs. So, let's roll up our sleeves and discover how we can leverage job crafting to help our clients turn the challenges of the VUCA world into opportunities for growth and satisfaction.

II. Understanding Job Crafting

A. Origins and Theoretical Background

The concept of job crafting has revolutionized how we think about

THE COACHING CORNER

work design. I still remember the first time I encountered this idea, it was truly a light bulb moment! Job crafting emerged as a formal concept in the early 2000s, challenging the traditional top-down approach to job design. Instead of managers dictating every aspect of a job, this new perspective suggested that employees could proactively reshape their work to improve their experience and satisfaction.

The idea of job crafting didn't just appear out of thin air. It's rooted in our understanding of how we process social information at work and what motivates us. Think about it, we're constantly interpreting our work environment and our attitudes and behaviors are shaped by this context. Job crafting taps into our need for autonomy, our desire to feel competent and our drive to connect with others. It's about taking some control over our work lives, rather than just passively accepting whatever comes our way.

The theory behind job crafting is fascinating because it's built on some fundamental truths about human nature. It's like a perfect storm of psychology, sociology and workplace dynamics coming together. Here's what makes it so powerful:

First, it acknowledges that we're not robots: we're meaning-makers. Just like we naturally customize our homes to reflect who we are, we have this innate drive to personalize our work experience. Every day, we're taking in information about our work environment, interpreting it and using these interpretations to shape our attitudes and behaviors. Job crafting gives us permission to be active participants in this process rather than passive observers.

Second, just like how a plant naturally grows toward sunlight, we humans similarly gravitate toward conditions that help us thrive. Job crafting taps into three core human needs that I've seen make a huge difference in people's work lives:

1. **Our need for autonomy:** that feeling of having some control over our destiny. When we can make even small choices about our work, it's like opening windows in a stuffy room.
2. **Our desire to feel competent:** that satisfaction of knowing we're good at what we do and getting better. Job crafting lets us align our work more closely with our strengths and areas where we want to grow.
3. **Our drive to connect with others:** that fundamental human need to build meaningful relationships and feel part of something bigger than ourselves.

What I find most beautiful about job crafting is how it honours both the individual and the organization. It hits that sweet spot where your unique talents, interests and values can create more value for everyone involved.

The best part? Job crafting isn't some complex theoretical concept that only works in academic papers. It's a practical, accessible approach that anyone can start using today. Whether

THE COACHING CORNER

you're a CEO or an entry-level employee, you have the power to shape aspects of your work to better align with who you are and what you care about.

B. Types of Job Crafting

Types of Job Crafting: Making Your Work Work for You

This is what I've learned about job crafting. It's honestly one of the most powerful tools we have to make our work more meaningful and enjoyable. It's like being an artist, but instead of sculpting clay, you're shaping your job to fit you better. Let me walk you through the three main ways you can do this.

First up is task crafting and frankly, this is where the magic starts! I had this idea that lit me up inside. I could create a feedback chatbot to help parents support their kids with homework. While I still used my teaching and organizing skills, I added something I deeply cared about which was bringing families together through learning. My heart would soar every time I saw a parent's face light up after mastering a new educational tool they could use with their child. My job became so much more than just teaching in the classroom. By following what mattered to me, I created bigger waves of change. The parents gained confidence with technology, the kids got more support at home and I got to teach in a way that truly excited me.

Reflect on what truly excites you at work, whether it's solving intricate challenges, fostering strong teams or innovating to improve systems. By intentionally weaving more of these passions into your daily tasks, you enhance not only your job satisfaction and personal growth but also inspire those around you. As you engage more deeply with what ignites your passion, you'll amplify your impact on the organization while nurturing your own development and well-being.

Then we have relational crafting, which is about reshaping who you work with and how you connect with them. I transformed my professional impact by reimagining my work relationships. I started looking at collaboration in a whole new way. I was the architect who was designing bridges between teams and departments. I didn't want to stay limited to my usual circle of teammates. Instead, I started building connections with leaders across different departments and even reached out to industry partners.

These new connections opened up exciting possibilities. I discovered insights from other teams that helped solve problems in my own work. My broader network meant I could connect colleagues with the right experts when they faced challenges. Soon, what started as my personal initiative grew into an informal knowledge-sharing network that helped everyone work more effectively. This is what we call a Networked Learning Community. By expanding who I worked with and how I interacted with them, I turned everyday conversations into opportunities for collaboration and growth. The impact of my work multiplied because I wasn't just focusing on my immediate tasks, I was helping build bridges across the institution where I worked.

THE COACHING CORNER

Think about what excites you most about connecting with others at work. Maybe it's mentoring, problem-solving together or learning from different perspectives. When you actively shape your work relationships around these interests, you create value that ripples throughout your organization.

The third type is cognitive crafting, and this one's my favourite because it's like putting on a new pair of glasses to see your role differently. It's amazing how changing your perspective can transform work you've done countless times before. I started seeing my daily work as pieces of a bigger picture. Those regular team meetings. They became opportunities to spark innovation. Routine project updates transformed into chances to connect different teams' work and create unexpected solutions. Even basic data analysis took on new meaning when I viewed it as uncovering insights that could shape our institution's future. By shifting my mindset, tasks I had done hundreds of times suddenly held new potential.

Think about how you view your role. Could those routine tasks actually be launching pads for innovation? Might those regular interactions hold untapped potential for positive change? When you reframe your perspective, you often discover new ways to create impact, even in the most familiar parts of your job.

Here's what really excites me about job crafting: you don't need permission to start making your role more impactful and you don't need to change positions to feel more fulfilled. It's about taking your current role and gradually reshaping it to better serve your community while aligning with your personal strengths and values. Sometimes the smallest changes can start a ripple effect of positive change.

Maybe you start by having one meaningful conversation with someone from another team, or by looking at a routine task through a fresh lens. Perhaps you add one new element to your weekly meetings that aligns with what energizes you. These small shifts might feel modest at first, but they create ripple effects. That new connection could lead to an innovative project six months from now. That fresh perspective on a routine task might inspire your whole team to work differently. The key is to start small, notice what works and let your impact grow naturally. Think of it like compound interest where each small positive change builds on the others, creating momentum and opportunities you might not even imagine yet.

C. Benefits of Job Crafting

The benefits of job crafting are numerous and, in my personal experience, can be truly life-changing. For employees, job crafting often leads to increased job satisfaction. When you shape your job to better fit your strengths and interests, work naturally becomes more enjoyable. Not only does job crafting make work more fun, but it also helps you feel less stressed. If you're doing tasks that you're good at and that you care a lot about, everything just feels easier. This balance makes your whole life better, not just your work

THE COACHING CORNER

life. You start to feel more positive and content in both areas. I've seen it boost well-being too. People who craft their jobs often report feeling more fulfilled.

Job crafting can also bring greater meaning to your work. By job crafting, you can shape your role to focus more on what truly matters to you. For a school teacher, it could be helping students discover their passions and achieve their potential. So, if you find joy in one-on-one interactions, you might design more personalized learning plans or offer extra tutoring sessions. This not only makes your work more rewarding but also helps students in a more meaningful way. When you align your tasks with what you find personally significant, even the challenge of motivating students can become deeply fulfilling. By aligning your tasks and interactions with what you find personally significant, you can transform even a seemingly mundane job into something deeply rewarding. The corollary is that when you find meaning in your work, your performance naturally improves.

Hence, job crafting can significantly enhance your career trajectory. When you actively shape your role to align with your strengths and interests, you're more likely to excel and stand out in your organization. I've seen professionals who engage in job crafting become the go-to experts in their niche, opening doors to exciting opportunities they might never have encountered otherwise.

But it's not just employees who benefit. Organizations have a lot to gain from encouraging job crafting. For one, it leads to increased

THE COACHING CORNER

employee engagement. People want to feel that they have some control over their work and when they achieve that, they're more likely to be invested in the outcomes. Another benefit is job crafting can also make an organization more adaptable. In today's fast-changing work environment, having employees who can proactively adjust their roles is a huge asset. It encourages employees to identify inefficiencies and suggest improvements. This proactive approach can lead to innovative solutions that enhance organizational agility.

Moreover, job crafting can be a powerful tool for staying relevant in a rapidly changing job market. By continuously adapting your role and expanding your skills, you're future-proofing your career. And here's something I find particularly exciting: job crafting can boost your innovative potential. In the process of reshaping your role, you often discover new ways of doing things. This not only makes your work more interesting but can position you as an innovator in your field. I've witnessed countless professionals revitalize stagnant careers and find renewed purpose through thoughtful job crafting. The beauty of job crafting, in my view, is its win-win nature.

While job crafting offers significant benefits, it is crucial to ensure that it aligns with the organization's strategic objectives. By providing guidelines or frameworks, companies can empower employees to craft their roles in ways that support broader organizational goals. This balance ensures that personalization does not come at the expense of collective aims. As you explore

THE COACHING CORNER

coaching for job crafting, keep these foundations in mind. Understanding the types and benefits of job crafting will help you guide others more effectively in reshaping their work experiences for the better.

III. The Coach's Role in Facilitating Job Crafting

Working with a coach can make job crafting more powerful and successful. Here's how a coach can guide you on this exciting journey:

First, a coach helps you spot hidden opportunities in your work. They bring fresh eyes to your situation and help you see possibilities you might have missed. When we're deep in our daily work, it's hard to see all the ways we could grow. A coach helps you step back and spot these golden chances.

Next, coaches are experts at helping you discover your unique strengths and true interests. Sometimes we're so used to our own talents that we don't even notice them. Or we might think our passions don't belong at work. A coach helps you uncover these hidden treasures and find ways to use them in your job.

Coaches also help you set clear goals and create smart plans to reach them. They guide you in creating goals that are both exciting and achievable. Then they help you break these big dreams into small, manageable steps. This makes your job crafting journey feel less overwhelming and more doable.

THE COACHING CORNER

Finally, coaches provide the support and accountability that keep you moving forward. Job crafting isn't always easy. There will be challenges along the way. A coach stands by your side, offering encouragement when things get tough and celebrating your wins when you succeed. They ask important questions that keep you focused and help you push past your comfort zone.

Remember, job crafting is an ongoing journey. As you grow and change, your job can grow and change with you. A coach can be your trusted guide on this path, helping you create work that truly matters to you and brings out your best.

Think about your own career journey. Are you using all your strengths? Does your work align with what matters most to you? These questions are just the beginning of creating work that truly excites and fulfils you.

As we explore the journey of job crafting, it's worth considering the value of professional guidance. While self-reflection is undoubtedly powerful, the insight and structure provided by a skilled coach can significantly enhance your job crafting efforts.

Bear in mind that job crafting is a skill that must be developed over time. With practice and persistence, you can become adept at continually shaping your role to align with your changing interests, strengths and career aspirations. The techniques we've explored here are not just tools for a one-time change, but skills you can use throughout your career to ensure your work remains meaningful and engaging.

THE COACHING CORNER

"Life isn't about escaping the darkness; it's about learning to shine in the shadows."

Where to find me:

LinkedIn - www.linkedin.com/in/ghazali-bin-abdul-wahab-75176130

THE COACHING CORNER

Chapter 17

By Amy Fong

Background and Early Life

Growing up in a large, middle-income Chinese family shaped my life in ways I still carry with me today. Our school holidays were not about lavish overseas trips but about the simple joys of childhood-playing with friends in the neighbourhood, cycling through streets, and making up games at the playground. These carefree moments taught us the value of imagination, community, and resourcefulness. In our diverse community, we shared festive seasons, celebrated each other's cultures, and built bonds that transcended differences.

Whether it was the lanterns of the Mid-Autumn Festival lighting up the streets or the scent of homemade dumplings during Chinese New Year, each celebration was an opportunity to come together,

THE COACHING CORNER

learn, and grow. To this day, the fragrant smell of curry will remind me of the food shared with my neighbours as they celebrated their festivals. This vibrant, multicultural upbringing instilled in me a deep respect for tradition, a love for storytelling, and an appreciation for the strength found in diversity.

This was a time before mobile phones and endless digital distractions. Socializing meant meeting face-to-face, laughing over stories, and being present in the moment. The path ahead was straightforward: study hard, secure a stable job, and start a family. I followed this road diligently, eventually discovering a fascination with technology that led me into a career with computers. I loved the solitude of working with a terminal—just me and the code, a quiet rhythm that resonated deeply. The simplicity of those early digital days held a certain charm, one where every line of code was a small triumph and every solution a step toward mastery.

Interestingly, I now understand why today's younger generation cannot seem to part with their devices; the pull of connection and control is familiar. My career took off in the financial sector, bringing opportunities to travel, experience diverse cultures, and savour local cuisines. While I thrived in technology, an unexpected curiosity about the human mind and behaviour began to grow, eventually steering me toward the field of psychology and coaching. It was during these travels that I observed how people from diverse backgrounds approached problem-solving and resilience, sparking a desire to understand the deeper layers of human thought and emotion.

What began as a technical journey soon transformed into a personal one. The more I delved into technology, the more I realised that beneath the algorithms and data lay a profound connection to human needs—efficiency, communication, and understanding. This revelation ignited a passion for blending my technical expertise with the human element, leading me to mentor others. Whether coaching colleagues on navigating corporate challenges or offering guidance on personal growth, I found fulfilment in helping others unlock their potential. My close friends make a joke about it, saying it is my journey from not talking to talking to humans. I am extremely fortunate that my family is very supportive in my pursuit to be a coach.

Today, my journey feels like a tapestry woven from two seemingly different threads: technology and psychology. Both fields, in their unique ways, are about solving problems, creating clarity, and fostering connections. The evolution from a terminal's quiet rhythm to the dynamic conversations of coaching has been transformative, and I have learned that the greatest insights often emerge when we blend logic with empathy. This ongoing journey reminds me that growth is not a destination but a continuous process of learning, adapting, and sharing.

The Turning Point

Life in the financial sector wasn't without its challenges. Balancing

THE COACHING CORNER

a career and family was often hectic, though mostly fulfilling. However, one experience stood out—a toxic workplace that tested my resilience. I worked under a manager who embodied the worst kind of leadership: gender-biased, verbally abusive, and relentlessly critical. It felt like no matter how well I performed; I was met with unwarranted scrutiny and negativity. Even when I was right, acknowledgement was absent or worse questioned to undermine my confidence. The relentless pressure wore me down, making even small victories feel hollow and short-lived. My confidence began to erode, replaced by a nagging sense of inadequacy that clouded my professional and personal life. Research studies have shown the effects of stress on the human both physically and mentally, and the impact not just on yourself but also all those close to you. As the saying goes, it is not something I will wish on my worst enemy.

The daily grind became unbearable, with every morning shadowed by the dread of another demoralizing day and evenings marked by stress and exhaustion. Work-from-home wasn't an option then, so escaping the toxicity felt impossible. Eventually, I sought help and connected with a compassionate psychologist who equipped me with tools to cope and reclaim my mental well-being. With her guidance, I learned to navigate the situation without letting it consume me. I began to recognise my boundaries, assert my worth, and gradually rebuild my self-esteem. The power of therapy and self-reflection opened my eyes to the strength that comes from vulnerability and the necessity of seeking support when the weight of life becomes too much to bear.

Though the work environment improved with new management, I decided to move on, recognizing the importance of prioritizing my mental health and career growth. That experience, though painful, was transformative. It sparked a desire to understand what drives such behaviour and how people can overcome its impact. This led me to pursue undergraduate and postgraduate studies in psychology while working full-time – a journey of countless weekends spent learning, reflecting, and growing. I also took courses and trained to be an accredited coach. Every new chapter of study deepened my empathy and refined my understanding of how resilience can be cultivated, even in the face of adversity.

Today, I integrate insights from cognitive-behavioural therapy (CBT), positive psychology, and other evidence-based approaches into my coaching practice. My experience taught me that there is always a light at the end of the tunnel, and it's okay to seek help along the way. Each client I work with is a reminder that struggles are not only obstacles but also opportunities for profound transformation. Through sharing my story and guiding others, I continue to reaffirm my belief that resilience, self-awareness, and compassion are the keys to thriving in both work and life.

Building My Dream

I believe my dream of building a successful coaching business can be done because I am passionate about helping others unlock

THE COACHING CORNER

their potential, and I know that passion fuels persistence. I have the skills, insights, and empathy to guide clients toward meaningful transformation, and I trust that the value I provide will resonate with the right people. Others have built thriving coaching practices from scratch, and their success proves it's possible with commitment and effort. Most importantly, I believe in my ability to learn, adapt, and grow, making this dream a reality step by step.

My coaching philosophy is rooted in the belief that every person possesses untapped potential waiting to be discovered and nurtured. Growth, resilience, and fulfilment are not abstract ideals but achievable realities within everyone's reach. My role as a coach is to help individuals unlock this potential through evidence-based strategies, collaborative exploration, and deep respect for their unique journeys. I passionately believe that change doesn't happen in isolation; it's born out of meaningful conversations, thoughtful reflection, and a willingness to embrace discomfort as a catalyst for growth.

I approach coaching with a strengths-based perspective, focusing on what's already working well and how those strengths can be harnessed to drive progress. Often, people underestimate their own abilities, focusing instead on their weaknesses. By shifting the narrative toward their existing capabilities, we create a foundation of empowerment and self-belief. Blending insights from positives I can share with future clients.

Together, we clarify core values, identify actionable steps, and navigate obstacles with curiosity and compassion. Self-awareness forms the foundation of my approach. Through reflective dialogue and tailored exercises, clients gain a deeper understanding of their thoughts, emotions, and behaviours, empowering them to make decisions aligned with their authentic selves. By building this awareness, they develop clarity not only about their goals but also about their motivations, strengths, and areas of growth. This heightened understanding allows them to tackle challenges with confidence and to make meaningful, sustainable changes in their lives.

Adaptability is another cornerstone of my practice. Each client is unique, and I tailor my approach to honour their cultural background, personal aspirations, and specific needs. Coaching is not a one-size-fits-all solution; it is an evolving process that respects individuality. By staying informed about the latest research and maintaining a reflective practice, I ensure that my methods remain dynamic, relevant, and impactful. Whether it is helping a client overcome self-doubt, navigate a career transition, or improve their relationships, my approach is always flexible and personalised to foster real, lasting change.

In building my dream as a coach, I have embraced journaling, mindfulness, and goal-setting frameworks as core tools for my own personal growth and resilience. For example, I use journaling to reflect on my daily progress, explore challenges, and celebrate small wins, which keeps me connected to my vision. Through mindfulness practices, such as morning meditation or deep-

THE COACHING CORNER

breathing exercises, I stay present and centred, allowing me to approach each task with clarity and focus. Additionally, I rely on goal-setting frameworks like SMART goals to break my dream into actionable, achievable steps-for instance, setting a timeline to complete my coaching certifications while carrying on my full-time job before embarking on starting a coaching business. These practices not only enhance my growth but also serve as powerful strategies I can share with future clients.

Over the years, I have had the privilege of working in partnership with clients from all walks of life - entrepreneurs, corporate professionals, students, and individuals in transition. Each client brings their own unique story, and every session is an opportunity to explore a wide range of topics and questions. From overcoming limiting beliefs to finding clarity in complex decisions, I have seen clients reach powerful conclusions and discover answers to problems that once seemed insurmountable. Their journeys remind me daily that coaching is not just about solving problems; it's about empowering people to trust themselves, take action, and create the lives they truly desire.

My ultimate goal is to empower individuals not only to achieve their dreams but also to cultivate lasting confidence, resilience, and well-being in all areas of their lives. When clients walk away with a stronger sense of self, a clearer path forward, and the resilience to face future challenges, I know we have accomplished something meaningful. Coaching, at its core, is about transformation-and I am honoured to be part of that transformative journey for so many.

Impact and Future Vision

If there is one regret I hold, it is that I did not embrace coaching sooner. Looking back, I often wonder how different my journey might have been had I had someone to guide me through my own crossroads, helping me uncover hidden potential and navigate life's complexities. During times of workplace adversity, career uncertainty, or personal struggle, a mentor's presence could have shifted my perspective, allowing me to face challenges with greater clarity and resilience. Now, as a coach, I am passionate about being that guide for others-helping them untangle the threads of doubt, identify their strengths, and move forward with confidence. Whether it is overcoming workplace toxicity, transitioning into a new career, or seeking personal development, I am committed to walking alongside my clients as they forge their path.

My vision is simple yet profound: to help people rediscover their strengths, embrace change with courage, and build lives that reflect their deepest values. Too often, individuals are caught up in routines that no longer serve them, held back by fear of the unknown or feelings of inadequacy. Personally, I have experienced all this in my corporate life and know how frustrating it can be. However, through my coaching practice, I aim to create a space where they can challenge those limiting beliefs, redefine their goals, and step into their potential. This is not about short-term fixes-it is about planting seeds of transformation that continue to grow long after our sessions end. Every breakthrough my clients

THE COACHING CORNER

achieve creates a ripple effect, empowering not only themselves but also those around them-family, colleagues, and communities.

I envision a future where coaching is accessible to all, not just those in leadership roles or high-powered careers. Personal growth should be a universal pursuit, and coaching can be a powerful tool in helping people from all walks of life unlock their full potential. As I continue to evolve in my practice, I am committed to expanding access to coaching through community initiatives, online platforms, and partnerships with organisations that value human development. By breaking down barriers, I hope to reach individuals who may not have considered coaching before, showing them how transformative it can be.

In the coming years, my goal is to integrate new technologies and methodologies into my coaching practice to ensure it remains relevant and impactful in a rapidly changing world. From digital tools that enhance self-reflection to AI-driven insights that personalise the coaching experience, the possibilities for innovation are endless. Yet, at the heart of it all, my focus remains on the human connection-the conversations that spark change, the trust that fosters growth, and the shared journey toward self-discovery.

Ultimately, my mission is to leave a lasting impact that transcends individual sessions. I want my clients to walk away with more than just solutions; I want them to gain a renewed sense of purpose, a toolkit for resilience, and the confidence to lead lives that are bold, meaningful, and aligned with their values. Coaching is not just

THE COACHING CORNER

about reaching a destination—it's about transforming the journey, and I am honoured to be part of that process for so many.

Feedback from clients reaffirms my mission, and I really want to continue to help others and make a positive impact.

"I am deeply grateful for the support and guidance you provided in helping me overcome my work stress. Your empathetic listening and tailored approach made me feel understood and empowered throughout our sessions. The practical tools and strategies you shared have not only helped me manage my stress but also improved my productivity and overall mindset.

I particularly appreciated how you encouraged me to set boundaries and prioritize self-care, which has made a noticeable difference in both my personal and professional life. Thank you for your patience, encouragement, and the actionable steps that have truly transformed how I approach my work challenges. You've made a significant impact, and I'm so glad I had the opportunity to work with you!"

Unlock Your Full Potential – Start Your Journey Today!

Are you ready to take control of your career, enhance your well-being, and build a life you're truly proud of? Whether you're a young entrepreneur charting your path, navigating the complexities of a new or mid-career stage, or seeking balance while overcoming personal challenges, I'm here to guide you every step of the way.

Together, we'll:

- Clarify your career goals and aspirations.

THE COACHING CORNER

- Develop actionable strategies to achieve success.
- Strengthen your resilience and mental well-being.

Your journey to confidence, clarity, and success starts with a single step. Book a consultation today and let's create the roadmap to your brighter future.

Let's build your tomorrow, today!

Linktree: https://linktr.ee/asimplepartnership

THE COACHING CORNER

Chapter 18

Review. Release. Reclaim. Reboot.

By Elsa Farouz-Fouquet

Holistic Wellness Coach and Practitioner

The Noisemaker

My name is Elsa, and I can scream-sing "Let it go" like nobody's business.

I am French on paper. I am a fast thinker, writer and definitely an emphatic speaker. I carry empathy and my funny bone with me. I have an annoying superpower: regenerative 7-minute naps. I also have Attention Deficit Oh Shiny! and raging dyscalculia. I need a GPS everywhere I go.

It seems my life's path involves walking through fire, shedding a tear or two, laughing some of my way out, learning a lot, and using that

THE COACHING CORNER

to guide others through their trials. Helping people feel better in every way is what makes me tick. We are all gloriously imperfect, shaped by our stories, talents, perceptions and flaws. Light and shadow co-exist in all of us, and I find that fascincting.

Allow me to take you on a journey of change.

I was born into a family of restauranters, the youngest of three, in a time when kids were meant to be quiet, obedient and invisible. There was love but also a lot of self-reliance and clear don't rock the boat commands: Be a good girl. Don't ask questions. When big people speak, small people stay quiet. My "favourite"? 'You sound like a noisemaker'.

To this day it baffles me when people say my voice soothes them during our sessions and my hypnosis audios help them fall asleep.

At age 8, I told my mother I'd live abroad, and that she'd have to look after my children. A few months later, the whole family moved to London. Coincidence, I promise! A year later, my parents began an 8-year-long divorce saga, and we returned to France.

I left again as soon as I could - armed with two degrees in Business and English. I built a life in the UK, trained as a language teacher and later as a trainer in the corporate field. I had my two daughters. 22 years and countless adventures later we are back in France, speaking English at home.

Review

I was taught to be dutiful and compliant despite a strong, vibrant personality. Inside, I felt like a volcano hovering over rivers of sadness. It wasn't okay to be me. I could always "do better", or "be better."

When that happens to you, my lovely, you grow up with a buried sense of whom you really are. It is buried deep, and it can give some people a chameleon-like ability to function, while others just act up. In both cases, it means that you don't get to grow, or tend to your own healthy boundaries. Not even with the people close to you. *Especially* with the people close to you.

So, what's it gonna be? People pleaser or Rebel?

Unbeknownst to my aware self, I became a people pleaser in most settings.

I met my husband at 19. Quiet. Confident. A symbol of peace after a slightly messy childhood. He wasn't the sharpest, and definitely slow at making decisions, but I thought my shine was enough for both of us.

He was critical. I knew I wasn't perfect, so I worked hard at being more of this and less of that, always relying on my "look on the bright side of life" tendencies.

When he scolded me, I would clap back with my usual flair. I was often right but nothing ever changed. Still, I felt I was standing up for myself. He would threaten to get angry. I was flexible to a fault.

I didn't know what gaslighting or stonewalling was back then, but I had a constant sense of unease like I was missing something...

THE COACHING CORNER

You're meant to feel good with your family, aren't you? I bent over backwards to make life work, grateful for even crumbs of kindness, relying on myself only, asking for very little.

I was a - scream with me: dumbass blind piece of SERIOUSLY WAKEUPWOMANANDLEAVETHATKNUCKLESCRAPER!

But I had babies.

I'd suffered a massive loss of identity when I wasn't allowed to work after being sent to China for his job. Then to India. And back to China. I was "a trailing spouse". Never mind that I was a qualified teacher and trainer, volunteer single-handed editor of a magazine for expats, that I had learned Mandarin on the spot, that I was a good friend, that I taught myself to decorate amazing cakes, that I was a good mother, or that the girls were turning out amazeballs...

He would ask me what my added value was. I didn't know anymore, he would brush off any valid answer. He even avoided physical contact and only ever looked me in the eye when he was trying to intimidate me if I was getting gobby.

My life had turned into a never-ending cycle of making sure the girls were ok, enjoying having a maid (perk!), trying not to die from Delhi Belly, telling people off in Mandarin for touching my babies in the middle of bird flu, finding THE brand of butter The Knucklescraper would agree to eat, keeping his personal snack cabinet well stocked with his favourite cereals, and hunting bloody Pink Lady apples because he wouldn't eat any other kind.

THE COACHING CORNER

I was a shadow of myself at home, with a wonderful social life and amazing friends outside. And I was still counting my blessings. I started reviewing my life.

Release

People couldn't understand what I was doing with him. He was bland in society, good at his job, quick on the blame trigger when he was put on the spot, forever a victim of my many shortcomings. He was toxic, and at the time I hadn't fully understood my need for safety and calm had led me straight into the snare of a familiar controlling environment.

The ugly truth came crashing down when my eldest was 12. After one of his fits of rage, she lay on the sofa, looked me in the eye, and said: "I know I can't have a strong man because he can hurt me."

That was the hardest hitting limiting belief I had ever heard. And it was coming from my baby. It was a truth she had internalised and voiced in front of her little sister, who was old enough to take it in.

All that time trying to keep the peace, finding him excuses, while knowing deep down that something was majorly wrong...

I was disempowerment personified.

I didn't have enough light to beat his shadow.

We were stuck in a toxic cycle of psychological and financial abuse. I felt complicit. It had to stop.

That night I asked the girls to give me two years. I couldn't slip out

THE COACHING CORNER

the back, Jack, or make a new plan, Stan, and I definitely couldn't get on the bus Gus, because I would have been caught at the China-HK border and sent to prison for kidnapping my girls, because he received an SMS the second I spent any money with a bank card. No plane tickets. No "I'm going to my sisters to think". We were stuck in China.

If I was going to make it out alive, I was going to have to release a lot, reclaim little old moi, and go for a full reboot.

I started studying.

I had a house in France, where my teaching qualification wasn't valid. I had to have something to offer after 11 years of being a trailing spouse. I knew people felt good around me, so I went for Aromatherapy and Hypnosis, which were always fascinating to me.

I sorted out a huge amount of our physical and emotional health issues and started helping others.

Because I had covertly learnt Reiki in India to level two, I was soon combining Reiki with oils, empathy, my funny bone and hypnosis. I threw in Mindscaping, studied that vagus nerve, EFT and then some. They are some of the building blocks of my work.

Gradually, I felt parts of myself come back online. My voice once dismissed as a "noisemaker," now comforted others. I discovered my ability to cut through people's pain and guide them to clarity and peace, using tried and tested tools and techniques.

That's who I was.

THE COACHING CORNER

As I started believing I wasn't (just) the worthless, worst mistake my husband had ever made, I worked on my shadow parts: co-dependency, lack of boundaries, self-blame, true and learned powerlessness.

Reclaim

I believe everyone needs to go through the same process, whichever tools they use.

I realised I had the opportunity and the ability to impact others while speaking with them while massaging them and making them laugh.

I could be me, and they could too. As long as there was someone to focus on, my ADD was dormant. I was efficient. I was damn good at getting to the root of issues, and finding solutions, facilitating change.

When you haven't really been taught to love yourself, and you have been conditioned to think you are "less than", you just float around, trying to be someone, anyone.

But let me tell you, when you decide you're going to finally reclaim yourself, it's glorious!

Whatever I was doing, he wanted me to stop. He sat me down one day. Before he could open his mouth, he was informed that if it was about any of my choices around coaching and healing, it wasn't open for discussion. He was so taken aback, he didn't go into the spontaneous combustion I was always in fear of.

THE COACHING CORNER

And so we kept going, but I had some money towards the start of divorce proceedings coming in.

Two years after the raging incident, the girls and I left for our usual summer of peace, family and friends in France. I'd lost my voice four months prior, making it impossible for me to work - it's like my body was trying to tell me something huh huh-. We didn't celebrate our arrival. We were just exhausted.

We had security cameras after a burglary. He would check on us via the app multiple times a day, listening to conversations, and joining in all the way from China. In a normal happy family setting maybe that would be fun, but it wasn't. He would chastise me if I had left the table uncleared and demanded we left doors open so he could see into the next room. I didn't know if he had hidden small gadget cameras too, my voice wasn't really coming back, probably for fear of saying something incriminating...

Then one day the girls and I found ourselves whispering at the bottom of the stairs with the doors closed so he couldn't see or hear. That's when I paused.

What the heck was happening? I thought I was getting free. It felt like a bad movie. He was 9500 kilometres away, yet we were still modifying our behaviour. He still had control.

Reboot

I sat the girls down and told them the time was now. It had been two years, I wasn't ready, but we had an opportunity to remain safe

THE COACHING CORNER

in the house. I couldn't get done for kidnapping.

I deregistered them from their habitual school so their residency visa in China would be voided.

I laid out a 4 phase plan that involved some lying by omission. There was very little bear poking for our safety. There would be no talk of "divorcement" as my little one called it.

That plan is valid for everything you want to do or create in life:

- A valid why.
- Asking for what you want or at least informing others.
- Making space and time.
- Using all the tools, getting and accepting all the help.

Phase 1: A 100% valid "why": my eldest needed to stay in France so she could reorient towards vocational training, because of severe dyslexia and no interest in "higher" education. He could take his sweet time finding another job.

That didn't go down too well but my resolve was iron-clad. I went back to China with him as the girls started school in France, picked up winter clothing and brought our cats over.

Phase 2: Asking for a divorce over the phone after he was back at work. Not pretty, but again, safety. In all plans, there must be a safety element. Distance was ours.

Phase 3: Making space for a reboot. In moments like these, before a major change, you need the right mindset and heart set so you can reboot your life.

THE COACHING CORNER

It may feel like an overwhelming chaotic void, but it's the perfect space to create the life or project you want. It's usually my clients' favourite part of the work once we have worked on releasing unhelpful beliefs and reclaimed their power.

Some coaches will tell you it's *all* about mindset. If you want something badly enough, you'll achieve it. Blah-blah-blah.

Others will preach systems and discipline, or the infamous "fake it till you make it."

That's some serious gaslighting if you ask me. And gaslighting is the last thing anyone needs.

How do you fake feeling alive when you're dead inside, you've built a life on someone else's beliefs and your essence has been sucked out?

How do you fake being ready to climb that mountain when you're weak at the knees and all you want to do is sleep for a hundred years?

No. It's not a case of not wanting it bad enough. You're feeling like you've only just come to, and your world has to change yet again.

- **The very first thing to do is to make a safe space and time for your reboot.**

Most of the time, and if you can, it starts with removing yourself from the situation. The environment has to change. I kept going for two hard years while reclaiming myself thanks to a strong "why."

THE COACHING CORNER

It took another two years of hunkering down to reclaim myself after my return to France.

I was in a loop about him. I couldn't drive for more than a half hour without having to stop for a nap. My girls ate a lot of home-made soup because that was all I could muster. Not all situations are this extreme, thankfully.

You'll have to do what you can, my lovely. And slow is perfectly ok.

Thou shall not blame thyself for thy 100% being only 20% or even 5% of what thou wish to give.

Rebooting is likely to feel pretty crap, scary and draining. But it's for the right reasons. That's the space and time where Life gets better.

Remember this, always: we want to trend towards better. There is no magic wand, only a spiral. You want to go up. You will slide down sometimes on some topics. Just do your best to trend upwards.

Lastly, here are some of the tools to get you started on your reboot:

- **You are a box of Lego:**

Imagine you are a big box of mixed toy building blocks. Some pieces are original Lego, some are the cheap fake blocks that don't quite fit with the real original. If you press the pieces hard enough, you can build some pretty decent stuff, but you know the pieces don't belong together.

When you don't know who you are anymore, you can't tell which piece of your environment, behaviours, beliefs, thoughts, emotions,

THE COACHING CORNER

or identity is original.

What I suggest you do is check each piece one by one and check if it's the real deal. The real you. It doesn't matter where you start, or in which area of life. Maybe you do like having too many cushions on the sofa. Maybe you don't want to eat at 7. Maybe you could go to the swimming pool again. Maybe you're a night owl. Maybe you like this or that style. Review every topic. Keep what's authentically you and toss what isn't.

Be gloriously selfish and self-aware.

Have a box of "not quite sure" pieces and reexamine them later.

Toss what is not serving you.

- **Be clear about what you want and why you want it:**

Even if you have no idea how to start your new project (yet). Whatever your project ends up being, make the decision, speak it out loud, write it down, paint it, sing it, and do your thing.

Reverse engineer whatever you want to achieve. Start with the end in mind. What do you want?

What are the factors hindering progress? (Be honest, it's not all about others)

Decide to feel better. KNOW that things always improve.

If you're not ready, rest a little bit more, but keep the idea and the feels you want to feel alive.

If people around you tend to belittle your ideas or project their limitations onto you, keep them for yourself for as long as possible.

- **Show yourself maximum compassion:**

Allow yourself moments of weakness.

Don't should on yourself.

Pick yourself up. Go at it again. Baby steps.

Allow yourself to rest.

You're busy relearning how to be, not do. The last time you did that may have been when you were a child before adults crushed you into a shape that was never meant to be yours.

- **Remember joy:**

Reflect on your happiest moments. What made them so? Don't fall into the Pool of Nostalgia and Melancholy, you're looking for the good stuff you can pull good vibes from. Now's not the time for a list of what was of what you've lost.

Do some of the stuff you used to like doing when you were a child.

Write shit down. Chances are if you have trauma, your memory is a bit wonky, so you'll remember happy things and forget three minutes later. Remember not to speak down to yourself if that happens.

- **Avoid:**

Toxic people and attention-stealing distractions.

THE COACHING CORNER

Situations that don't float your boat.

Any binge of any kind. OK, the odd chocolate binge maybe, but nothing that alters your consciousness, you need your head screwed on tight.

Sad or aggressive movies and music.

- **Increase:**

Sleep. Rest. Snoozing. Pillow cruising. Getting stuck between your duvet and your top sheet. Checking your eyelids for cracks.

Good nutritional decisions. Your freezer is your best friend on wonky days. If it's made in a factory or keeps for a very long time, chances are it's nutritionally void and will push you towards junk food.

Exposure to nature. Trees offer a great connection. Sand and dirt get stuck between toes, but they do wash off.

Exposure to animals, people and things who make you feel good. In that order, maybe?

Saying no. Granted, that's a hard one. People will not be happy. But then again, are they ever really happy? Huh? They'll get used to it. You know Bob at the office, who said no so many times that no one asks him to do stuff anymore? Be like Bob. (Try not to burn bridges, I know you get my drift).

- **Reignite your senses:**

Use color therapy. Wear red underwear and spice up your decor.

Eat vibrant foods. And I don't mean dyed foods...

Scream-sing in your car, pump up that music, get dancing.

Do weird stuff like saying hi to drivers going in the opposite direction in silly voices.

- **Anchor good feelings:**

Squeeze your wrist when you feel joy.

Write about it like a recipe for future happiness.

Use uplifting (natural) essential oils.

Tell people you love that you love them.

Write down your wins. Read them regularly.

These are a few of my favourite things. There is a lot more available to you. More tools, more techniques, more ways of handling what life has thrown at you.

Once you've steadied yourself somewhat, seek support. You've got this. You've done all those things for yourself and by yourself. There is no way you are "less than". You are enough, at the very least.

Coaching isn't about being "fixed". It's about rediscovering yourself, reclaiming your life, and moving forward. It's about teaming up with someone you can trust, someone who makes you feel seen and heard, someone who knows how it feels and has come out of the other end with stories to tell.

Are you ready to try something different and release what no

THE COACHING CORNER

longer serves you, reclaim the parts of yourself you've forgotten, so you can reboot your life with purpose and joy?

Do you have a project you want to put together, but the voice inside is not quite sure you can make it? Are you ready to be more you and to feel good about it?

Let's navigate this journey together. With empathy, humour, and proven tools, I will guide you to rediscover your strength and design a life that feels authentically *you*.

Elsa Farouz-Fouquet

Holistic Wellness Coach and Practitioner

Your next chapter starts here. Let's write it together.

Linktree: https://linktr.ee/ICanFeelGreat

THE COACHING CORNER

Chapter 19

By Emma Leivesley

Wellbeing and Burnout Coach

From Burnout to the Beginning

I woke up one cold, wet, grey and miserable Monday morning in February 2014, and I had nothing. I felt nothing. I felt as if somebody had scooped out my soul and left an empty shell. I lay there in bed with my eyes open, completely numb. I did the only thing that I could think of to do. I called my boss, and I told her, "I'd rather kill myself than come in to work today".

The thought of going through another day winging it, another day pretending I was OK, another day of impossible demands, another day of IT problems, another day of pretending that I cared. I had absolutely nothing. There was no way that was happening.

I was teaching creative media at a college. Chronic stress and

THE COACHING CORNER

exhaustion from the impossible targets, the meetings being told that despite how hard we were working, we weren't good enough, and the endless paperwork that in no way benefitted us or the students. I wanted some sleep. I hadn't unclenched my jaw in four years.

That was the end of my eight-year teaching career.

I got a minimum wage job working as a mental health support worker. Here I was dealing with actual life and death situations, and this was less stressful than the meaningless targets that we were made to feel were life and death working in education.

After a permanent position, I worked for an agency in secure units, prisons and psychiatric hospitals and saw a lot of unseeable things, but I loved it. The only problem was, in a lot of cases, it was like my first day. I had some shifts in places that felt familiar and was familiar to other staff and service users, but the other shifts, I just felt awkward. I realised just how much confidence I'd lost. That woman who had confidently stood up in front of classes told jokes and taught cool stuff was a distant memory. The work became sporadic, and I needed something more secure but temporary while I finished my MSc Psychology dissertation.

A job was advertised for a GP receptionist. I'd done this before after I left school. It had been on the old paper system and now everything was digitised, but it would soon come flooding back I thought.

It took three years to recover from burnout. During my darkest days when I was between teaching and support work, I was reading a book giving an overview of psychological theorists which I'd bought for £3. I read about Ellis and Beck and Cognitive Behaviour Therapy and having had CBT myself I realised that psychology could save me. Psychology and neuroscience gave me the ability to think my way out of anything.

In 2020, my squiggly career compass took me back to working in mental health as an assistant practitioner at the same GP practice. Having been a qualified hypnotherapist for ten years, and with a son with a degenerative neurological condition needing a bungalow, I focussed on my private practice to make more money.

Then coaching came along. I realised what a powerful force of good coaching is, and I completed my coaching and NLP training. Working in a team of amazing colleagues from a range of professions and specialisms in healthcare, I could see how much people were struggling. My coaching business was born.

I'm Emma Leivesley, and I help stressed out doctors, nurses and allied professionals get work-life balance and calm with wellbeing and burnout coaching.

Stress Vs Burnout

In order to understand what burnout is, it's important to define what stress is. Everyone feels stress, we even need stress. Eustress is a form of stress that we need to motivate us: it's that burst of cortisol (the stress hormone) that we get in the morning that gets

THE COACHING CORNER

us out of bed. If we didn't feel healthy stress levels, there would be no sense of urgency to tackle tasks that need doing and we wouldn't be able to hold down jobs or progress in our careers. I wouldn't be sitting here typing this book chapter.

Unhealthy stress however is when we don't feel able to cope or when the stress response is triggered too often. Chronic stress is when we're under stress for a long time and we're living in survival mode. I'll explain what's going on during the stress response.

The hypothalamus is part of the brain that acts like a control centre for a lot of our bodily functions such as heart rate and hormone regulation. When we feel stressed, it gets a message from the amygdala, which is our brain's security guard, that something bad is going down. This causes the sympathetic nervous system to switch on. The sympathetic nervous system is part of our in-built survival mechanism and when activated, it gets our bodies ready to deal with a threat.

Evolutionary, this was a massive advantage as we regularly encountered predators: we had to do something to get rid of the bear that was about to attack us. Enter, the fight or flight response, courtesy of the sympathetic nervous system. Adrenaline and noradrenaline are surging through your bloodstream and causing your neurons to fire in your brain to activate/deactivate a range of systems. This increases your heart rate and blood pressure, and breathing becomes fast and shallow. It also shuts off the prefrontal cortex: the bit of the brain that does the rational thinking, meaning that once the fight or flight response has kicked in, you're less in control of your emotions, your powers of reasoning and judgement have left the building, and you're going to lose perspective of the situation as you cope with the immediate "threat". Unfortunately, the amygdala is very shouty and can be easily triggered as it can't tell the difference between a real threat (like a bear), and a perceived threat (like an angry boss, a missed deadline, or looking at your work email inbox after having two weeks off).

The idea is that we fight the bear and defeat it, we run away from the bear (flight), or the other option: we freeze or fall on the floor and hope the bear doesn't eat us, thinks we're dead and goes off to do bear stuff. We've got rid of the threat, and then the parasympathetic nervous system is allowed to drive the bus. This is our "rest and digest" mode where our blood pressure, heart rate and respiratory rate reduces back to normal. We get normal brain function back so can reflect and reason with what has just happened. We think "Oh my days, a bear... I'm glad I got away".

If the bear is particularly good at running, and the sympathetic nervous system is still doing its thing, the body needs to get some energy from somewhere- adrenaline and noradrenaline will run out. Our helpful control centre, the hypothalamus, releases corticotrophin and the pituitary gland releases adrenocorticotrophic hormone. Their combined efforts push the adrenal cortex (in the adrenal glands atop the kidneys) into releasing corticosteroids. The energy comes from the liver so the bear chase can continue. When we either get killed and don't need any more energy, or we successfully avoid the bear and can rest-

THE COACHING CORNER

the lovely parasympathetic nervous system has its time to shine.

Brilliant. But what if your amygdala has triggered this response for a stressful situation at work or at home? There may not be an end to that bear chase, so this keeps on going. When the liver is pumping out energy, the immune system is suppressed. Your resting heart rate and blood pressure will be higher which can cause a whole heap of problems such as a greater risk of cardiovascular disease, heart attack and stroke. Prolonged stress is very, very bad for your physical health.

If stress goes unmanaged, it leads to burnout. Your body can't release that energy anymore, so you feel exhausted, unmotivated and like you have nothing left to give- remember the morning I woke up feeling like my soul had been scooped out. Burnout is very, very bad for your mental health. It takes a long time to recover from. A lot of people use the term "burnout" when they mean stress. How do you know the difference?

Stress causes physical symptoms- racing heart, inability to relax, insomnia, hypertension, muscle tension and headaches. You may be worrying or anxious and could develop a generalised anxiety disorder or have panic attacks. If you were to go for a nice couple of weeks away, you'd likely feel a lot better. Burnout causes psychological symptoms- irritability, resentment, apathy and depression. There is a higher risk of suicide. A nice couple of weeks away wouldn't help very much. If I had time off work when I was teaching, I would spend those two weeks vomiting and sleeping as my body tried to adjust to not being under an immense amount of pressure. That was a sign I really shouldn't have ignored. Burnout prevention really is better than cure.

Because there is a high prevalence of burnout in healthcare workers, there is a higher prevalence of suicide. In the UK, doctors are twice as likely to die by suicide than the general population. Female doctors are 76% more likely to end their own lives. We lose one GP every four weeks to suicide. Nurses are struggling too and also have a high suicide rate.

When I heard these horrific statistics, it really upset me. All these wonderful people who have dedicated their lives to helping people and gone through years of difficult training are being worked to death. Healthcare professionals are being taken advantage of the world over because they care, want to help and don't want anyone to come to harm. I'm passionate about helping them manage these stress levels because these lovely people deserve to have happier, calmer lives and live to have a bloody amazing retirement.

Healthy Daily Habits

Stress needs managing before there are physical health problems or it leads to burnout. Don't just plough on through. I learned that lesson the hard way. If the check engine light is on, check the engine. While working full time in a GP practice, processing complex trauma spanning 26 years, and working a lot on my business as I was the only member of the household working, I ignored the insomnia, constantly clenched jaw and all the advice that I give to everyone else. My blood pressure was 199/139 (for

THE COACHING CORNER

those who don't know, that's what us folks in healthcare call "really f**king high"), I had chest pain radiating to my jaw and left arm, a headache, my eyes felt like they were going to explode and all the capillaries in my nose were on fire. After two nights in accident and emergency and two weeks off work, I had to reassess. Stop when you get the early warning signs, or your body or mind will choose when you stop, and it won't be convenient.

You are not a genetically modified super-doctor, a robot nurse or a supernatural being. Self-care is an absolute essential for every single human and you need to activate that parasympathetic nervous system regularly and break the stress cycle. Having daily healthy habits means that you do this on autopilot without thinking.

Good habits include:

- Having a healthy diet and keeping sugar, salt, alcohol and processed rubbish to a minimum.
- Daily exercise- breaking up sitting behind a desk by going for a 15-minute walk is a great way of doing this. If the weather is awful, do something else. A colleague and I found a belly dancing tutorial and did this in the office. Do a few squats in between patients. Use your massive water bottle as a kettlebell. Do whatever works for you.
- Daily mindfulness- this is doing anything where your attention is focussed on the present. This could include meditation, yoga, gardening, playing music or whatever you like doing that allows you to become completely

focussed. There is a free guide about this on my website listed at the end of the chapter.
- Laughing- I swear by this. Laughter makes life so much easier to cope with. I have a rule- make at least one person laugh every day.
- Get your glimmers in. A glimmer is the opposite of a trigger. A trigger is something that causes a specific symptom of a mental health condition or brings back a horrific memory. A glimmer is something that makes us feel good and connected with other people, or that we have purpose. Aim for 5 a day like with fruit and veg. You can keep a tally of this. It could be something like someone saying thanks or giving you a compliment, having a funny interaction with someone or feeling like you've really helped someone. If you've not reached 5, engage in glimmer seeking behaviour. Go and compliment someone, do a random act of kindness or telling your partner or relative that you love them.
- Practice gratitude- as I type this I recall when I used to want to tell people to piss off for suggesting this, but it really does work. Rather than focussing on what's gone or going tits up, it's good to train your brain to focus on what's going well. It could be writing down 3 things you're grateful for, ringing someone up and saying thanks and that you appreciate them or focussing on aspects of yourself that you like. I'm often taken aback at my ability to get through absolutely f**king anything, and I like that I can think on my feet, and

THE COACHING CORNER

that I genuinely care about people. It might help to go and get a piece of paper and write down all the attributes of you that you like.

Your Perfect Day Off

I want you to think about a perfect day off. This is a day off in the realms of possibility. You're not in the Bahamas and a magical £1,000,000 deposit hasn't been made into your bank account. I want you to think about:

- What time you'll wake up
- What you'll do when you wake up
- Where you will go and what you will do
- Who will be with you (it's really ok if you want to be alone)
- Work your way through the whole day until you go to bed

Be specific and let your imagination run with it. Write this down and underline the key activities.

Now try to make three of those things happen a week as a minimum.

Non-Negotiables

You have to be strict with yourself on this one. These are things that you absolutely will not negotiate on. These things are happening and nobody, not even yourself, will stop them from happening.

I recommend having a daily, weekly and monthly non-negotiable. Some of the examples I'm about to give aren't realistic or possible

THE COACHING CORNER

in everybody's situation so pick something that's realistic and relevant for you.

Examples of a daily non-negotiable:

- A 15-minute walk in your lunchtime
- Reading the kids a bedtime story
- Daily workout
- Reading before bed
- Finishing work on time (I can sense some of you laughing- I did say they're not all realistic for everyone)
- Time spent on a hobby

Examples of a weekly non-negotiable

- Go to boxing training- that one is highly specific to me
- Finish work on time on a Friday (I can sense that laughing again- especially from those of you who work in a GP practice)
- Weekly date night with your partner
- Watching your favourite programme
- Hiking up a mountain

Examples of a monthly non-negotiable:

- Monthly date night with your partner if weekly isn't possible
- Payday trip to the cinema
- Going out with a friend

THE COACHING CORNER

- Hiking up a mountain for people who don't want to go hiking every week
- Spa day (I wish I could do this once a month- how amazing would that be?)

The Future

I've just told you about a lot of things and that's all well and good, but if you don't take action and do the things, they won't work. How many times have we read about what we should be doing but we don't do them? I want to make these things easy for you to do and realistic so it's really important that you reality check your non-negotiables. I don't want to make you feel like you've left mandatory stress training at work. If you've ever been to one of these, you may have left swearing.

This takes practice to build up so you may want to focus on one aspect at a time. Another thing I want you to remember is that stress management and burnout recovery is possible, even if it really doesn't feel like it now. I haven't always been as chilled out as I am now, and I get stressed because I'm a human. I once got thrown out of a Tai Chi class for swearing. Now, some things bother me, they're bound to. All emotions are valid as they give us a message and tell us that something is wrong. The trick is to receive and interpret that message and then let go of the emotions that hurt us.

To help you track what you're doing, I've made a workbook which you can download for free by scanning the QR code at the end of this chapter or by going to my website. There will also be a recording of a webinar that you can watch which goes over the main points.

I dream of a future where people aren't having to work with the bare minimum resources, aren't being worked to death and are able to live calmer, happier lives. Unfortunately, I don't have much influence over government policy or your employer, but I can help you manage stress and avoid or recover from burnout. It's my life mission.

Your Mission

Your mission, if you choose to accept it, is to love your job and love your life without having the unhealthy kind of stress. I've helped people with a range of problems:

- I've helped an HCA become more assertive and confident to challenge poor patient care in their workplace- they did this and it got rid of a whole heap of stress
- I've helped so many doctors and nurses with a work-life balance audit and action planning session. One said, "I came at you with a whole load of problems, and you've turned them into three achievable goals"
- I've helped many healthcare professionals prioritise self-care, feel calmer, become more confident and tackle self-doubts
- I've helped a nurse with vicarious trauma process that trauma and not let it hinder them at work

THE COACHING CORNER

I use:

- Coaching
- NLP (neurolinguistic programming) - making changes in the unconscious mind
- Hypnotherapy
- Cognitive behavioural techniques
- Teaching mindfulness
- Meditation
- My geeky love of neuroscience
- Compassion, empathy and absolute commitment to helping you

I like to leave people floating out of sessions on a cloud of calm. I would love to help you feel calmer and happier. Your mission is my mission.

If you go to my website, you can download the free habit tracker accompanying this chapter and a free mindfulness guide.

You can also book a session or a free call to see if we're a good fit and how I can help you. I look forward to meeting you.

Website: www.programmes.emmaleivesley.com

Linktree: linktr.ee/emmaleivesleycoaching

THE COACHING CORNER

Chapter 20

The Ripple Effect

By Vicky Regan PCC, CEC

Leadership Coach for Women

The Spark that Starts it All

Every great achievement begins with a small spark of inspiration—a single moment or act of encouragement that grows into waves of change. This is the essence of mentorship: a ripple effect that transforms lives, careers, and communities.

How It All Began

For me, that spark came as a teenager when I joined the Civil Air Patrol (CAP), the auxiliary of the U.S. Air Force. CAP's cadet program emphasized aerospace education, leadership training, and search-and-rescue missions, but it instilled so much more:

THE COACHING CORNER

mentorship, integrity, and a commitment to serving others. It was this formative experience that ignited everything I've done since.

I joined CAP because of my uncle Jim. Universally loved, Jim a pilot with an infectious passion for flying and a remarkable ability to connect with others. As a child, I was captivated by his stories, humor, and his two-seater airplane, but what truly stayed with me is his kindness and unwavering encouragement. Jim has a way of making people feel seen and supported—a gift that profoundly shaped my own approach to leadership and mentoring.

At CAP, I was surrounded by people, friends to this day, who shared Jim's values: a commitment to lifting others, a belief in service, and a dedication to lead with integrity. These lessons were the foundation of my leadership experience. They planted the seeds of a lifelong belief that one small action—a moment of encouragement, a thoughtful conversation—can create ripples of impact far beyond what we might ever see.

The Career Connection

Years later, as I entered the professional world, I carried those lessons with me. But I quickly discovered how challenging it could be to navigate certain environments without representation or mentorship. At one company I worked for, only 7% of employees were women—yes, you read that right, 7%. It was an isolating experience, but it also became a catalyst.

I knew that I wasn't the only one facing these challenges. That understanding ignited my commitment to mentorship, particularly for women in male-dominated fields. Over time, I championed women's mentorship through organizations, launched Employee Resource Groups, and built internal mentoring programs. I founded an organization dedicated to empowering women in technology and worked tirelessly to create spaces where women could support and elevate one another.

This work has taught me one thing above all: when women support each other, the possibilities are limitless. Mentorship isn't just about one person guiding another—it's about creating a culture of empowerment where everyone has the opportunity to thrive.

Bringing It Full Circle

What started as volunteer work alongside my career evolved into my life's calling. The decision to center my career on leadership, mentorship, and advocacy for women has been the most rewarding shift of my life. Today, through my coaching practice, Hone Leadership, I work to help women unlock their full potential and redefine leadership for the modern workplace.

Mentorship is powerful because it's accessible to everyone. Unlike coaching, which is a credentialed practice, with mentoring you don't need a title, a credential, or years of experience to make an impact. It's about showing up, supporting others, and amplifying voices that might otherwise go unheard. The ripple effect of mentorship is real—and when women support women, we don't just take our seats at the table. We transform the entire room.

THE COACHING CORNER

Let's Get Started

This is about more than mentorship—it's about the legacy you create when you choose to lift others as you climb. Together, we'll explore the ripple effect of mentorship, why it matters, and how to make it meaningful. Whether you're just starting or looking to deepen your impact, you have the ability to create ripples that will inspire and empower generations to come. Let's dive in.

Mentors: Building the Case for Mentorship

Mentorship is one of the most accessible ways to create a lasting impact—on your mentee, your organization, and yourself. Mentors don't just guide others; they learn, grow, and evolve through the process.

6x Women mentors are **promoted six times faster** than those who don't mentor (Forbes)

They report improved leadership skills, enhanced communication, and greater career satisfaction. Beyond professional advantages, mentoring provides deep personal fulfillment:

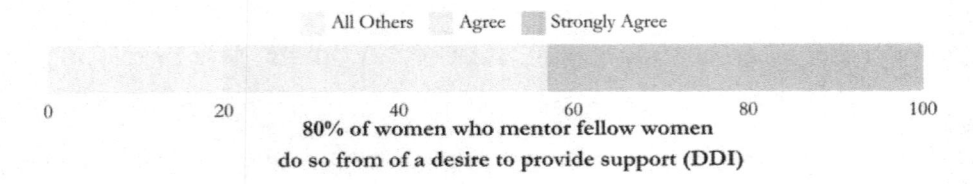

All Others | Agree | Strongly Agree

0   20   40   60   80   100

80% of women who mentor fellow women do so from of a desire to provide support (DDI)

This underscores how mentorship serves as a catalyst for connection and empowerment.

THE COACHING CORNER

When I reflect on my own experience as a mentor, I've found that I often learn just as much as I share. My long-term mentorship with Julia perfectly exemplifies this. She's smart, empathetic, and a natural leader—an absolute pleasure to support. Honestly, she's also just way cooler than I ever was, even on my coolest day. Watching her grow in confidence, tackle challenges, and thrive has been one of the most rewarding experiences of my career. At the same time, her insights and fresh perspectives have given me renewed optimism for the future of women in the workplace. The ripple effect of mentorship is undeniable: empowering one person sparks a chain reaction that enables them to uplift others in return.

What Are the Benefits?

Mentoring is a reciprocal relationship that sharpens leadership and communication skills for mentors while providing mentees with guidance, confidence, and access to opportunities. Unlike coaching, which centers on the client, mentoring benefits both parties. Mentors often report that teaching reinforces their own knowledge, while exposure to new challenges or ideas sparks innovation.

Research highlights mentoring's transformative impact:

87% of both mentors and mentees report greater confidence and empowerment as a result of their partnership (HBR)

THE COACHING CORNER

Many mentors describe feeling more connected, inspired, and energized through these relationships, contributing to inclusive, growth-oriented workplace cultures.

Why Aren't More Women Mentoring?

Despite mentorship's clear benefits, not enough women step into mentoring roles due to two key challenges:

- Apprehension from mentees: Many hesitate to ask for mentorship.
- Self-doubt among potential mentors: A perceived lack of technical expertise holds them back.

79% of working women do not feel confident enough to ask for a mentor (KPMG)

Frequency that women have been asked to be a mentor (DDI)
54% have been asked only a few times or less in their careers
20% have never been asked

71% of women always accept invitations to be formal mentors at work

It's important to address this gap. Research shows mentees value leadership guidance over technical expertise. They seek support in navigating challenges, building confidence, and growing into leadership roles—areas where women mentors excel.

Mentors don't need all the answers; they just need to listen, provide perspective, and guide mentees through critical thinking and self-discovery.

Best Practices for Great Mentors

THE COACHING CORNER

Being a great mentor isn't about being perfect—it's about being intentional, empathetic, and supportive. Here's how:

What to Do:

1. **Build Trust:** Create a safe space where your mentee feels comfortable sharing challenges and aspirations.
2. **Ask Questions:** Encourage critical thinking, problem-solving, and self-reflection by asking, "What approaches have you considered?" or "Can I share an observation?"
3. **Provide Honest Feedback:** Frame feedback as a constructive and actionable tool for continuous growth.
4. **Set Goals:** Encourage your mentee to set SMART goals and celebrate milestones along the way.

What to Avoid:

1. **Overstepping Boundaries:** Respect your mentee's autonomy; guide, don't dictate.
2. **Making Assumptions:** Avoid projecting your experiences; every journey is unique.
3. **Being Inconsistent:** Follow through on commitments to build credibility.

Great mentors adapt their approach to meet their mentee's unique needs, empowering them to uncover solutions. Mentorship isn't just about shaping someone else's experiences—it's about growing together.

THE COACHING CORNER

By investing in others, you not only enhance your own leadership but also create ripples of positive change that extend far beyond the relationship.

Make a True and Lasting Impact

We've discussed the best practices of being a successful mentor—building trust, listening actively, and providing honest feedback. As effective mentors, our primary focus is guiding our mentees through their challenges and helping them navigate solutions. However, to provide an even greater and more lasting impact, there are foundational topics you can weave into your mentorship that will always serve your mentee as they grow in leadership. These topics transcend specific scenarios and equip your mentee with critical skills for long-term success: communication, executive mindset, and feedback.

1. **Communication: Clear, Concise, and Impactful**

Mastering communication is the cornerstone of effective leadership. It's not just about what you say but how you say it—and how it resonates with others. By helping your mentee refine their communication, you empower them to inspire confidence, build trust, and lead with clarity.

To simplify the path to leadership communication, focus on these three pillars:

THE COACHING CORNER

Powerful presense	Straightshooter	Positive
Limit expressions of negativity and self-doubt. Confidence inspires trust and credibility.	Say what you mean and mean what you say. Direct, clear communication eliminates ambiguity.	Authentic positivity builds confidence in others and creates a supportive environment.

As a mentor, model these behaviors in your own communication, and challenge your mentee to practice them in their daily interactions.

2. Executive Mindset: Thinking Comprehensively

One of the most critical shifts for emerging leaders is moving from tactical thinking to strategic thinking—from being in the weeds to getting in the treetops. This shift, known as developing an executive mindset, involves seeing the big picture, aligning decisions with broader organizational goals, and anticipating future challenges.

Help your mentee embrace this transition by:

- Encouraging them to regularly step back and assess their role within the larger context of their organization.
- Guiding them to ask questions like, "How does this decision align with long-term goals?" or "What are the potential downstream effects?"
- Supporting them in developing patience and resilience, as this mindset shift from tactical to strategic is a process that takes time and consistent effort.

THE COACHING CORNER

An executive mindset is about thinking comprehensively, balancing short-term execution with long-term vision, and building the confidence to navigate complexity. By helping your mentee make this shift, you prepare them for higher levels of leadership.

3. Mastering Feedback: Giving and Receiving

Feedback is the foundation of growth, adaptability, and coachability. As a mentor, teaching your mentee to give and receive feedback effectively is one of the most valuable skills you can impart. Why? Because feedback isn't just about improvement—it's about unlocking potential.

Coachability, the ability to seek, receive, and act on feedback, is a proven driver of success. Highly coachable individuals are:

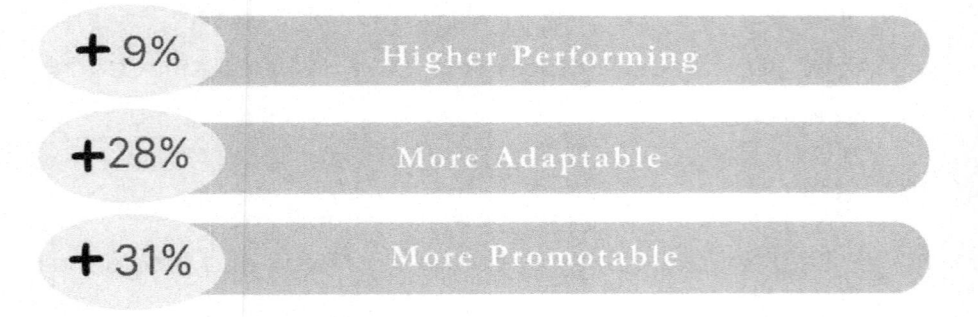

- **+9%** Higher Performing
- **+28%** More Adaptable
- **+31%** More Promotable

Help your mentee develop a positive relationship with feedback by:

- Showing them how to seek it proactively. Questions like, "What's one thing I could have done better?" can open valuable conversations.

- Emphasizing that feedback is a gift, not criticism. Encourage them to view it as an opportunity for growth.
- Teaching them how to deliver feedback that is direct, actionable, and constructive. Frame feedback as a way to empower others rather than to criticize.

As a mentor, model openness to feedback yourself and share your own experiences of how receiving tough feedback helped you grow. This is one of the most important areas you can help your mentee develop and well worth your time and focus.

Women don't typically receive guidance or training in these critical areas. As a mentor, focusing on these foundational topics, you'll help your mentee build essential leadership skills that will serve them throughout their career.

Mentees: Leveraging Mentorship to Unlock Your Potential

The data is undeniable: mentorship is one of the most powerful tools for professional growth.

Women with mentors **earn 20% more** and are **promoted five times faster** than those without (Forbes)

75% of professionals credit mentorship as crucial to their career development. (ATD)

94% of employees with mentors report greater job satisfaction. (LinkedIn)

THE COACHING CORNER

56%

Only **56% of companies offer internal mentoring programs,** leaving many women to navigate finding a mentor on their own. (DDI)

So, how do you find the right mentor? And once you do, how can you build a successful relationship that drives results? Let's explore practical strategies to help you identify, approach, and work with a mentor to unlock your full potential.

Why Mentorship Matters for Mentees

Mentorship provides both tangible and intangible benefits. Studies show that mentees are five times more likely to be promoted and report higher levels of confidence and empowerment. Beyond career advancement, mentorship offers guidance, encouragement, and a trusted sounding board for navigating challenges. It's an invaluable resource for career growth and personal development. However, mentorship is not a passive experience. To reap its benefits, mentees must take an active role in shaping the relationship. A mentor can't walk your journey for you—but they can help light the path.

How to Find and Ask for a Mentor

Finding the right mentor starts with clarity. Reflect on your goals and identify areas where you need guidance. Are you navigating a career transition? Building leadership skills? Clarifying your long-

THE COACHING CORNER

Reverse mentoring pairs junior employees with senior leaders, offering guidance on emerging trends, technology, or cultural shifts.

This dynamic encourages cross-generational understanding and ensures leadership remains connected to modern practices and perspectives.

4. Leadership Coaching

Leadership coaching is a highly personalized, goal-oriented approach to growth that is 100% focused on your development vs the reciprocal nature of mentoring. By addressing specific challenges and refining leadership skills, coaching provides tailored guidance and accountability. It's designed to help you achieve measurable outcomes, build confidence, and unlock your full potential in navigating complex career paths and leadership opportunities.

5. Personal Advisory Boards (PABs)

A Personal Advisory Board (PAB) is a highly versatile and impactful support system. Unlike traditional mentoring, a PAB is composed of trusted individuals who offer diverse perspectives and advice on both personal and professional matters.

The structure of a PAB can vary widely. Some prefer a formal arrangement with quarterly meetings to review progress, discuss goals, and seek guidance. Others, like myself, take a more informal approach, relying on a small group of trusted advisors, personal leadership skill, and multi-generational teams—sometimes spanning five generations—have become the norm. These changes, combined with rapid organizational transformations, have created an urgent need for more diverse and adaptable support systems.

This is why cultivating multiple sources of support is more important than ever. Exploring innovative mentoring approaches can enrich the mentoring experience, offering fresh perspectives and strengthening the impact of these relationships.

Alternative Support Approaches

1. Community-Based Mentoring

Professional associations, industry groups, and local organizations are excellent platforms for connecting with mentors and peers. These communities provide collective learning, shared experiences, and a broad network of support that can accelerate personal and professional growth.

2. Peer Mentoring

Peer mentoring involves partnerships between individuals at similar career stages, creating a collaborative space to exchange insights, solve challenges, and hold each other accountable. This reciprocal approach promotes mutual growth and problem-solving.

3. Reverse Mentoring

THE COACHING CORNER

- Strategies for upcoming projects or goals.
- Skills you'd like to develop.

At the start of your mentorship, share your short-, mid-, and long-term goals to give your mentor a complete picture of your vision.

Regularly revisit these goals to ensure you're on track and adjust priorities as needed.

Sustaining and Evolving the Relationship

Mentorship is a dynamic relationship that evolves over time. Here's how to keep it thriving:

- **Celebrate Progress:** Recognize small wins and reflect on growth milestones together.
- **Embrace Feedback:** Ask questions like, "Are there blind spots you've noticed that I might benefit from working on?" and act on the guidance you receive.
- **Communicate Openly:** If the relationship begins to stagnate, revisit your goals and discuss adjustments.

A successful mentorship is built on trust, transparency, and mutual effort. When you take ownership of your development and show appreciation for your mentor's guidance, you create a partnership that drives meaningful results.

It Really Does Take a Village

The shift to remote and hybrid work has reshaped how we connect, collaborate, and lead. Emotional intelligence is now a critical

term vision? Knowing what you need will help you identify the best mentor for your development.

Once you've identified potential mentors, here are actionable steps to approach them:

- **Personalize Your Request:** Share your professional goals and why you value their expertise. For example: "I'm looking for guidance as I navigate [specific goals], and I believe your experience with [specific achievements] can offer valuable insight."
- **Be Clear About the Commitment:** Propose a manageable schedule, such as one lunch and one coffee meeting per month—either in person or virtual.
- **Offer Flexibility:** Acknowledge their busy schedule and express your willingness to adjust to their availability.

By being intentional and respectful in your approach, you're more likely to build a strong foundation for a productive mentor-mentee relationship.

Maximizing the Relationship

Your mentorship's effectiveness begins with you. Set the tone by preparing meeting agendas that steer the focus toward your goals. Share your topics with your mentor in advance to ensure meetings are efficient and aligned.

Consider discussing:

- Recent achievements and challenges.

and professional, who provide candid, actionable feedback as needed. Whether your PAB is formal or casual, personal or professional, or a hybrid of all, the most important factor is trust.

What makes a PAB so powerful is its ability to bring together varied viewpoints, which can help you approach challenges and opportunities from new angles. Over time, this can become one of the most enduring and valuable forms of mentorship, offering a ripple effect of growth and empowerment that continues throughout your career and life.

Expanding Your Support System

As workplaces continue to evolve, so must our approaches to mentorship. Today, it can be more than a single mentor—you can build a network of support that enables you to thrive, inspires others, and creates a lasting impact.

Mentorship and the Ripple Effect

We often don't realize the impact our words, actions, or guidance can have on someone else's life. Sometimes, it's a small piece of advice, a moment of encouragement, or simply being there as a sounding board. But when we take an intentional role—when we choose to mentor—we create opportunities for others to grow and thrive, sparking a ripple effect of transformation.

One of the most profound aspects of mentorship is its ability to multiply.

THE COACHING CORNER

89% of people who are mentored go on to mentor others (HBR)

Think about that for a moment—your investment in someone else's growth has the power to amplify across generations and industries. It's more than just a statistic; it's the tangible proof of the ripple effect in action. When women mentor other women, we're not just supporting individuals—we're helping to reshape the leadership landscape, address systemic barriers, and inspire real, lasting change.

For Mentors: Keep Going

Mentorship isn't just about the lessons you share—it's also an opportunity for personal and professional growth. It challenges you to sharpen your communication skills, expand your perspectives, and deepen your emotional intelligence. As mentors, we're reminded that leadership isn't about having all the answers—it's about asking the right questions and staying open to learning.

Personally, I still rely on mentors and my Personal Advisory Board (PAB) to navigate challenges, gain insights, and grow in my own leadership. These relationships have been instrumental in my development and are a testament to the lifelong value of mentorship.

When Mentoring Isn't Enough

There are moments in your career when a more focused, structured

THE COACHING CORNER

approach may be the key to breaking through challenges or elevating your leadership skills. This is where leadership or executive coaching can complement mentorship. Coaching provides tailored strategies, clear frameworks, and actionable insights to help you achieve specific goals and overcome obstacles. If you're considering this next step, it's worth exploring how coaching can help you thrive in your career and next steps.

Taking Action

Whether you're inspired to become a mentor, find a mentor, or create your own PAB, there's no better time than now to take action. This chapter is just the beginning; I have in-depth free resources that delve into every step of successful mentorship—from finding and asking the ideal mentor to setting up your partnership for long-term success. If you have questions or want additional guidance, I'm here to help. Visit www.honeleadership.com for mentorship insights, resources, or to start a conversation about leadership coaching.

The Ripple Effect Lives On

Mentorship is about more than individual success—it's about building something larger than ourselves. Every connection you make, every piece of wisdom you share, creates ripples that extend far beyond what you might imagine. By mentoring or being mentored, you're contributing to a legacy of empowerment that shapes industries, communities, and generations.

When we support one another, especially as women, we unlock

THE COACHING CORNER

potential, open doors, and illuminate paths for those who follow. That's the true power of mentorship: it's not just about impacting one life—it's about transforming the future.

Vicky Regan, PCC, CEC

Leadership Coach for Women and Founder

Hone Leadership

Website: www.honeleadership.com